By Ved Mehta

DADDYJI

Daddyji, England-Returned, 1921

VED MEHTA

DADDYJI

Oxford University Press

OXFORD NEW YORK TORONTO MELBOURNE

Oxford University Press

Oxford   London   Glasgow

New York   Toronto   Melbourne   Wellington

Nairobi   Dar es Salaam   Cape Town

Kuala Lumpur   Singapore   Jakarta   Hong Kong   Tokyo

Delhi   Bombay   Calcutta   Madras   Karachi

Library of Congress Cataloging in Publication Data

Mehta, Ved Parkash.

Daddyji.

Reprint of the ed. published by Farrar, Straus,

and Giroux, New York.

1.   Mehta, Amolak Ram, 1895-   2.   Health-officers
—Punjab—Biography.   3.   India—Social life and customs.
4.   Fathers—India—Biography.   I.   Title.

[RA424.5.M43M43 1979]   362.1'092'4 [B]   79-15154

ISBN 0-19-502619-5

Printed in the United States of America

I BEGAN MY AUTOBIOGRAPHY WHEN I WAS TWENTY. IT was my first book and was published three years later as "Face to Face." I have not read it in the fifteen years since, but I have often wanted to revisit the worlds it describes, for in retrospect it seems only a partial outline of the story I really want to tell. "Daddyji" is a part of that story, and is the first of a series of books I hope to write exploring my own history. Wherever the old and the new accounts overlap, there may be certain discrepancies or shifts in interpretation, but that is as it should be—the one was constructed only from the fragments of my memory, the other from the testimony of all the witnesses I could find to talk to.

I know no way of expressing here the gratitude I feel for the inestimable help of Amanda Vaill Stewart, Gwyneth Cravens, William Shawn, and Amolak Ram Mehta.

V.M.

New York
February 1972

CONTENTS

PHOTOGRAPHS

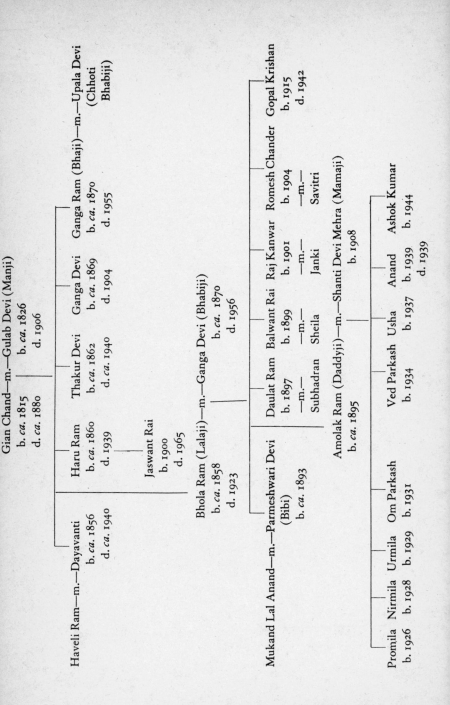

I

VILLAGE

I N WINTER, THE SKY IS BLUE AND HOSPITABLE, THE nights are frosty and starlit, the fields are left furrowed by the plow, and the air is filled with the call of partridges, the honking of wild geese overhead, and the languid creaking of Persian wheels as the bullocks turn them round and round to draw water from the wells. At the close of winter, Basant-Panchami—a festival honoring the god of work—arrives, and everyone celebrates it by wearing yellow clothes, flying yellow kites, and eating yellow sweetmeats; the fields become bright, first with the yellow of mustard flowers outlined by the feathery green of sugarcane, and later with maturing stands of wheat, barley, and tobacco. When the trees are loud with the buzz of bumblebees, it is time for the festival of Holi, celebrating the destruction of evil—when everyone's clothes are merrily splashed with red-tinted water. In summer, the earth is seared by hot, dry winds, the trees are stripped of their leaves and almost immediately clothed in blossoms, and the landscape is made rich with the crimson of cotton, the red of coral-tree flowers, and the scarlet of flame-of-the-forest. Then, while the mango groves echo with the crying of barbets and of Indian cuckoos, the heat of the sun, direct and relentless, bakes the plain, blanching everything except cactus and camel thorn. The rivers dry up, and dust storms swirl and sweep across the plain, turning it into a desert. Through the heat comes the cry of the brain-fever bird—"brain fever . . . brain fever"—and the still, moonlit nights are streaked with dark formations of geese fleeing to the cool of the mountains. In the monsoon at the end of summer, the pied-crested cuckoo appears, riding the monsoon wind from East Africa. Black clouds boil up from the southwest. Explosions of lightning and rumbles of thunder rend the clouds, and rain pounds the land. The rivers overflow, fields become mires, and snakes crawl and wriggle in the mud. The earth smells sodden, and mosquitoes whine everywhere. Finally, the pale sun breaks through the clouds ("the marriage of the lion and the jackal," the children call this union of sun and cloud), the air becomes heavy with the sweet, rich fragrance of mangoes, and leaves and grass sprout anew. In the autumn, the rains subside, the mud recedes, the cotton is picked, and rice, millet, maize, and lentils are sown. Then it is winter once more.

It was in this fertile, brutal land, in the Punjab, up and down the rivers and along their canals, that the family tree of the Mehtas sent down its roots and spread. The Punjab—in Hindi the name means "land of five rivers"—looks like a scalene triangle standing on its sharpest corner. The shortest side, on the north, consists of the Himalayan range; the longest, on the west, of the river Indus; and the third, on the east, of the Gangetic plain. The five rivers that give the land its name—mighty rivers all—rise in the mountains and flow down across the plain, dividing it into fertile tracts before converging and merging their waters with those of the Indus. The forebears of the Mehtas came from the village of Bhikhiwind, in an arid stretch of land bordered by the Ravi, the middle river of the five, but sometime during the reign of the Moghuls they moved upstream and resettled in the village of Nawankote, which was about thirty miles northwest of Lahore, the commercial and cultural center of the province. Nawankote consisted of flat-roofed daub-and-wattle huts hedged in by cultivated fields. Its most important landmark was an ancient banyan tree, where girls who were possessed by demons were strung up by their feet and swung from side to side while the village crier thumped on a drum, until the evil spirits were exorcised; sometimes the possessed girls died during the ordeal. Near the banyan tree was a mosque, whose *maulvi* (Muslim priest) was the wise man of the village. Villagers too poor to bring up their children often gave their sons to the mosque, and the *maulvi* brought them up. He fitted the little boys with iron skullcaps, and they grew to manhood with the heads—and the brains—of children. They managed to keep alive by trooping behind religious mendicants—begging and giggling—from village to village, and were popularly known as *Shah Daula ke Chuhe,* or Mice of Shah Daula. (Shah Daula was a Muslim saint associated historically with madness.)

The Ravi, like its sister rivers, overflowed regularly during the monsoons, taking huge bites out of the village land and devouring them. The river eventually swept away the local Hindu temple, and in the seventeenth century the Muslim proselytizers sent out by the Emperor Aurangzeb converted the inhabitants of Nawankote to Islam. In the time of my great-grandfather Gian Chand, Nawankote had about two hundred families, only four of which were Hindu; by caste, one was Brahman, one was Vaisya, and two were Kshatriya.

These Hindu families tenaciously guarded their ancient traditions. Every day, when a Vaisya or Kshatriya woman kneaded dough for the family meal, she would give a big ball of it to the family cow as a thank offering, and when she had finished baking the chapattis, she would give the first one to the Brahman's wife—who came for it regularly—as another thank offering. If the Brahman's wife had any of the bread left over, she would dry it and sell it back to her benefactors, who would then soak it in water, mix it with cottonseed, and feed the mash to the cow. The Brahman supported his family with these offerings and with what fees he received from officiating at weddings, births, head-shavings, and other ceremonies. The Vaisya family owned the village's only shop, which was stocked with wheat flour, crude sugar, salt, lentils, ghi, mustard oil, kerosene—the necessities of life. The two Kshatriya families—one was Gian Chand's and the other was his brother's—owned in common a bit of land, some cattle, and a couple of horses, and by village reckoning they were well-to-do. They leased their land, together with seed for planting and a pair of bullocks for plowing, to landless cultivators, who paid the brothers with a major share of the harvest.

One day, Gian Chand heard that a prosperous Sikh in the next village had gone to Lahore, bought some mill-made cloth—which had just started coming in from England—and given it to his daughter as part of her dowry. Gian Chand, who was noted for his enterprise, got on his horse, galloped to Lahore, purchased several bolts of English muslin and longcloth, strapped them to his saddle, and rode back to Nawankote, where he set up a little stall to sell cloth; it was the second shop in the village. He died sometime around 1880, and although he was survived by a wife, three daughters, and three sons, he left half his land, one of his two cows, and some of the family silks and jewelry to the Brahman, on the strength of an earlier promise that if Gian Chand made such a bequest, he would be reincarnated as a rich man with vast estates irrigated by canals of milk and honey.

Gian Chand's eldest son was in his twenties when he became head of the family and, consequently, responsible for the care of every last blood relative and for what family property there was. He was born a year or two after the Indian Mutiny of 1857. As a baby, he had an unusually trusting face and so was given the first name Bhola (Innocent). His second name was Ram, so that the god would be invoked whenever the child was called. When Bhola Ram was nine or ten, he began studying informally with the *maulvi*, who exhorted the child to give up temporary pleasures for permanent achievements. The *maulvi* taught the boy to read and write Urdu, and, with the help of primers and two books called "Gulistan" and "Bustan," gave him a little instruction in Persian and Arabic. But the child's education consisted mainly of memorizing the Koran and, to improve his calligraphy, copying out passages from it. At the end of the day, Bhola Ram would sometimes steal away and listen to the music of a group of nautch and singing girls who had their quarters just outside the village gate; they earned their living in nearby towns as entertainers to prosperous merchants. Now and again, the girls would give Bhola Ram lessons in playing the

tabla or the sitar. One day, when Bhola Ram arrived at
the mosque, the *maulvi* said, "What do I hear? It is written that dance and song have no place in Islam. Leave
the drums to the drummers." From that day on, the boy
shunned the company of the girls and redoubled his
study of the Koran.

Soon after Gian Chand's death, when the brutal
heat of summer was broken by the monsoon rains—a
deliverance that the villagers celebrated by going on
long visits—Bhola Ram went by ekka, a small, one-
horse vehicle, over the muddy roads to Lahore and
boarded a train for Amritsar. He arrived there a couple
of hours later and walked to the village of his maternal
uncle, who was so influential in the region that as a
matter of course he often played host to the district col-
lector. As it happened, Bhola Ram and the district col-
lector, an Englishman who took pride in his knowledge
of the local culture, were guests at the same time. The
Englishman was much impressed by the young man's
bearing and by the appearance of his Urdu script, which
was so elegant that it could have been used to make
lithograph plates for printing. Although Bhola Ram
lacked the formal schooling usually required for a government job, the Englishman offered him the position
of *patwari* in the Department of Canals and Irrigation.
A *patwari*, he explained, was a petty official who kept
tax records for a group of villages, noting down how
much acreage was under irrigation and how much
money the landowners owed the government for the
canal water they used. The job had some drawbacks,
however. In order to guarantee the *patwari's* official
objectivity, he not only was uprooted from his home

and sent to unfamiliar ground but was also transferred every three or four years. Even so, Bhola Ram, excited by the prestige of government service and the prospect of adventure held out by the frequent transfers, accepted the offer. For bureaucratic convenience, he took as his last name the name of his subcaste—Mehta.

When Bhola Ram returned from his visit to his uncle, he took an urn containing his father's bones and ashes—"the flowers," the Hindus call them—to Hardwar for immersion in the sacred river Ganga. He and half a dozen relatives and neighbors who were going on similar pilgrimages travelled in ekkas to Lahore. From there, they took a train southeast to Saharanpur, in the United Provinces, and from Saharanpur they walked thirty-five miles due east through jungles and marshes to Hardwar. There Bhola Ram went to a tenement in an ancient lane by the riverbank, and roused the *panda* (genealogist) who had hereditary rights over the Mehta subcaste; he and his itinerant *panda* brethren, from Mattan, in the Vale of Kashmir, kept records of the births, marriages, pilgrimages, and deaths of the families in their custody. After Bhola Ram had identified himself and made a cash offering to the *panda*, the *panda* unlocked a wooden cupboard, carefully removed from it a bundle of parchments, undid the cord that tied them, and, turning to the correct page, read out, "The Mehtas of Bhikhiwind at Manakpur near the well. Ram Jas Mal and Sahai Singh were the sons of Pardhana Mal and the grandsons of Budhwant Rai and the great-grandsons of Mansa Ram. The sons of Ram Jas Mal were Jawahar Mal, Karam Chand, and Amir Chand. The sons of Karam Chand were Gian Chand,

Khan Chand, and Bura Mal. Bhola Ram, Haru Ram, and Ganga Ram were the sons of Gian Chand, the grandsons of Karam Chand, the great-grandsons of Ram Jas Mal, the great-great-grandsons of Pardhana Mal . . ." He wrote on the page with a thick quill pen, "And Bhola Ram came with the flowers of Gian Chand." He recorded the place of Gian Chand's death and accompanied Bhola Ram to the steps of the sacred river. Along the way, Bhola Ram bought rice, ghi, and coconut, which the *panda* blessed and sacrificed to the Ganga. Then Bhola Ram scattered the flowers upon the water.

WHEN BHOLA RAM, or Lalaji, as he had come to be called—"Lala" is a sort of caste title, and "-ji" is a suffix denoting affection and respect—was about twenty-eight, the village Brahman of Nawankote heard about a marriageable girl from his colleague in the village of Burkhurdar, twenty miles away. The Brahman of Nawankote, with Lalaji in mind, began negotiations with the Brahman of Burkhurdar, who was able to satisfy the Brahman of Nawankote on several crucial points. The girl was from the same caste as Lalaji. Her people, like Lalaji's, were landowners and shopkeepers, but they were also moneylenders, and were therefore a little bit more prosperous. She was strong and healthy; she was five feet four (a little taller than most village girls); she had clear-cut features; and she was outstandingly beautiful. She was barely fifteen. The two Brahmans compared the horoscopes of Lalaji and the girl, and, finding them to be compatible, declared the match propitious. One day in early spring, Lalaji and his male relatives went on horseback and in ekkas to Burkhurdar for an elaborate wedding ceremony, which lasted three days. On the last day, as the Brahman of Burkhurdar chanted mantras over a sacred fire, Lalaji and the girl, whose face was covered by a veil (he was not to see her face until he had taken her back to Nawankote), walked together around the fire seven times, the groom renamed the girl, changing her name from Ganga Devi to Asa Devi, and they became man and wife. Then the bride was placed in a palanquin for the journey to her new home, in Nawankote. The palanquin was carried on the shoulders of hired bearers, with the bridegroom and the *barat* (bridegroom's party) riding on either side of it, and the old midwife who had brought the bride into the world walking alongside to comfort her. As the procession set off, Lalaji's younger brothers showered the palanquin with handfuls of small coins, which the local Untouchables and their families scrambled to retrieve. From time to time along the way, the procession would rest, and the old midwife would carry sweetmeats and water from the *barat* to her charge. When they reached Nawankote, the bride, having left her family and her village, took her place in her new family, where she was called simply Bhabiji (Elder Brother's Wife) by everyone except her husband, and her life, like that of every other relative, was defined entirely by her role in the family.

WOMEN FREQUENTLY DIED in childbirth, and their in-laws were usually blamed for their death, especially if the woman had shown signs of unhappiness in her new home. Since monogamy was the rule among the Hindus, it was not uncommon for in-laws who regretted their choice of daughter-in-law to let her die in childbirth, in the hope of getting a second daughter-in-law, with a second dowry. There were also instances of female infanticide—of a midwife's turning a girl child's face against the placenta, so that she suffocated in her mother's blood, whereupon the midwife was duly rewarded for having made certain that the girl she delivered was "stillborn." For such reasons, Bhabiji was returned to Burkhurdar for her confinements. As it happened, however, both her first child and her second were stillborn, and her third, to everyone's disappointment, was a girl. But sometime around 1895, in midwinter, Bhabiji gave birth to her fourth child, a son. He was my father. In order to ward off evil spirits, the midwife, as soon as she had cut the umbilical cord, passed the baby through an aperture in a special brass plate, took him to the family cowshed, and laid him in the manger. Meanwhile, one of Bhabiji's sisters climbed onto the roof of the room in which the baby was born, and poured mustard oil down the drain. A drummer, a flute player, and a sarangi player—the village band—paraded through the lanes, and alms were distributed to the poor. The Brahman of Burkhurdar chanted mantras over the baby, invoking the protection of Brahma. He then examined the palms of the baby's hands and the soles of the baby's feet, and cast the baby's horoscope; he created a great stir by declaring that the boy would grow up to ride upon the backs of elephants and sail upon the sea.

Although my father was named Amolak Ram, to

us, his children, he has always been known by the
hybrid name of Daddyji. During Daddyji's early years,
Lalaji was posted as a *patwari* to successive groups of
villages in the district of Amritsar. These villages were
little walled clusters of low, flat huts rising from the
ruins of their predecessors and surrounded by fields.
Between the fields and the village walls was a belt of
open space, where refuse was dumped, where bullock
carts were left, and where there was a pond for bathing
cattle and for soaking cart wheels to prevent their joints
from shrinking. Inside the village walls was a spider-
web of muddy lanes, off which doors opened into court-
yards. All these villages were on the Bari Doab Canal,
which had been completed in 1879 to irrigate thousands
of acres of barren land. Lalaji would make one village
in the group his headquarters after he had ascertained
that it contained an important local landowner who
would serve as an ally, that the family would be safe
from marauders who roamed the countryside, and that
there was a school nearby.

The first house that Daddyji can remember was in
Kathunangal. It consisted of a few windowless mud-
and-plaster rooms built around a partly covered courtyard and connected by passageways. In the front was a
long room, where the men of the family—Lalaji and his
brothers—slept. In the back were three smaller rooms,
of which two served as sleeping quarters for the children
and the women of the family—Bhabiji, her mother-in-
law, and Lalaji's sisters—and the third as a storeroom
for barrels of wheat and lentils and crude sugar. The
rooms were bare and dim, being lit in the evening by
the flicker of little mustard-oil lamps, and furnished

with a few low stools, many charpoys, and one big chest, which held bedding. Along the walls were wooden pegs on which clothes were hung. The only decoration was in the front room—an old calendar bearing a faded picture of Sita adorned with jasmine flowers and Ram and Lakshman carrying bows and arrows. The cooking, eating, and washing were all done in the courtyard, and the family animals—a saddle horse and a buffalo and a cow—were tethered there at night.

Bhabiji was always the last in the family to eat and the last to go to bed. She milked the cow and the buffalo, churned the milk to make butter, and drew off the buttermilk. She plastered the earthen floor every day with cow dung—it was both antiseptic and holy—and gathered twigs and cotton stalks, which, along with cakes of cow dung, were used as fuel. She prepared all the meals—vegetables, lentils, and chapattis—which the family ate sitting on stools or on charpoys around the hearth. Afterward, Bhabiji washed up—except for the brass pots, which were scrubbed by a boy servant.

As became a *patwari's* wife, Bhabiji always kept herself presentable, plaiting her hair neatly in a long pigtail, which she tied with a black woollen tassel or a black ribbon, and wearing a *salwar* and *kameez* (loose trousers and shirt) of white cotton, varied occasionally with stripes or checks, and keeping her head covered with a white veil; for weddings or festivals, however, she wore a red, yellow, or pink sari and plenty of gold jewelry. All the same, she was surprised if anyone paid attention to her. Daddyji remembers Lalaji giving her only one compliment: he once brought her a single narcissus. She thereupon exclaimed, *"Ik phul/Par lakh mul!"* ("One flower, but worth a million!").

For a time, Lalaji owned an office chair—the only one in the village—and he would sit in it when people came to call on him. When Bhabiji was a bride, she was cleaning around the chair one day and she sat down in it, perhaps merely to try it out. Just then, Lalaji's youngest brother, Ganga Ram, who was about her age, came into the room behind her and punched her in the back. "What are you doing in *his* chair?" he bellowed. She jumped up in alarm, and thereafter she always approached the chair with respect.

Although Bhabiji could neither read nor write, she was well versed in Punjabi proverbs, and she impressed upon everyone around her the virtues of detachment and discipline, of purity and generosity, of practicality and cheerfulness by means of appropriate sayings: *"Jehra ghariyahai/Us tutna vi hai"* ("What the potter has made must also break"); *"Dekh paraee chopri te nah tarsaeen jee/Rukhi missi khaeke te thanda pani pee"* ("Seeing another person's buttered bread, don't let your mind be disturbed; eat dry and nonwheat bread and drink water"); *"Mala teri kath di dhage laeepro man vich ghundi pap di Ram jape ki ho"* ("I have strung your prayer beads on a thread, but when the heart is impure, what is the use of invoking Ram?"); *"Wand khae so khand khae/Kalla khae so dad khae"* ("To one who shares food it is sugar; to one who eats alone it is a toad").

Whenever Bhabiji had a free moment, she spun

cotton yarn, singing the few songs she knew in a sweet, melodious voice to the hum of the wheel; later, she took the yarn to the village weaver, who wove it into bedding. Above all, she liked to sit with a length of coarse cotton cloth on her knees and embroider it in silk. She always filled the cloth with the same simple design, in red and yellow—a pattern of large squares, rectangles, or rhombs, the figures being repeated so that each one enclosed progressively smaller replicas of itself. Everyone thought Bhabiji painstaking in her embroidery except Thakur Devi, Lalaji's next-younger sister, who had been widowed at an early age and left with two daughters to support but no sons to comfort her in her old age. When she thought she spotted a crooked stitch in the needlework, she would rap Bhabiji's knuckles. Yet Bhabiji would defend her, saying, "Sister Thakur Devi is a perfectionist and a gifted seamstress. We should sympathize with her situation."

The unquestioned ruler of the household was neither Bhabiji nor Thakur Devi but Manji—Lalaji's mother. Manji got up in time to salute the sun as it rose, and she saw to it that everyone else got up then, too. (This was hard on Bhabiji, who couldn't doze off during the day, as Manji could and did.) Manji would then sprinkle water in the direction of the sun and chant:

> "There is one God.
> He is the supreme truth.
> He, the Creator,
> Is without fear and without hate.
> He, the omnipresent,
> Pervades the universe.
> He is not born,
> Nor does He die to be born again.

By His grace shalt thou worship
  Him.

"Before time itself
There was truth.
When time began to run its course
He was the truth.
Even now, He is the truth,
And evermore shall truth prevail."

Manji had a strong, pretty face, whose attractiveness
was actually accentuated by her wrinkles. She had rosy
cheeks, and as a baby she had been so fair that she was
named Gulab Devi (Rose Goddess). There was always
a musty smell about her from snuff; she frequently took
fastidious little pinches from a small silver snuffbox en-
graved with images of Ram and Sita, claiming that it
kept her breathing passages clear. She also took a small
black pill of opium every day. Her back was straight
and her gait steady, and when she was young she was
famous for being able to carry on her head three full
brass pitchers, stacked one on top of another, without
spilling a drop. At meals, she insisted that everyone take
only a small serving, and anyone who took a second
serving had to finish every scrap of it. If someone
dropped salt on the floor, she would scold him, saying,
"In the next incarnation, you will have to sweep up
with your eyelashes every grain you have dropped."

The only person whom Manji ever praised was
Lalaji. One hot summer night, when everyone in the
family was sleeping out in the courtyard, a thief somehow managed to steal a necklace that Manji was wearing. The necklace was a gold chain on which hung
sovereigns stamped with the head of Queen Victoria

and with the words "Guinea" and "Asharafi"—their denomination in English and Urdu—and it was her most treasured possession. She was inconsolable, but the very next day Lalaji ordered an exact duplicate of the necklace to be made for her. When she saw it, she called him "my Sharvan," after a legendary son who was so devoted to his blind parents that he used to carry them in the pans of a scale slung across his shoulders.

"You SHOULD COME OUT, like a mushroom, over-night, without anyone's knowing what you are doing until you appear in your full glory, and you should always sit at the head of the charpoy, so that you can dominate the person sitting at the foot," Lalaji was fond of saying. And, indeed, when he came home, usually late in the evening, he would sit at the head of his charpoy and draw on a brass hookah with a silver mouthpiece. He had been smoking a hookah since he was six, and there was an entire ritual connected with it: the hookah had to be frequently filled with glowing coals and fresh water, and its tobacco always had to be a special blend that had been cured in molasses. Lalaji was equally particular about his appearance. He sported a well-trimmed beard and a long, thick mustache, its ends turned up in the manner of his warrior caste. (The Kshatriyas were so zealous about the upward twirl that it was lowered only in defeat.) The beard and mustache, along with the prominent, high-bridged nose that all the Mehtas have, gave his face a magisterial look. He wore white calico pajama trousers and loose white twill shirts, and tied his turban, which was of the finest white

Lancashire muslin, high on his head, so that he looked taller than his actual height, which was five feet nine. He walked with his head up, his chin in, and his shoulders squared, and when he went out, he wore a black alpaca coat, so that no one could mistake him for a peasant—he and the *maulvi* were the only two villagers able to afford the luxury of a coat—and he was one of the first Punjabis to own an umbrella, which he holds proudly in an early photograph.

Lalaji always made sure that he had the best mount in the village—usually a mare, who would be mated to the best Arabian stallion in the district. Most of the day, he was out on his horse in the hot sun, collecting field notes for the *khasra*, the *patwari's* book of records. With the help of an attendant who carried a long iron measuring chain, Lalaji surveyed and noted down the acreage of land under irrigation; to avoid paying water rates, villagers sometimes irrigated their fields with canal water they channelled off surreptitiously. The *patwari* had to record the arable land correctly in the *khasra*, because the *zilladar*, who was in charge of between twenty and twenty-five *patwaris*, came regularly to check the book. Still, the *patwari* could record fields as having been unproductive of crops during a particular harvest, as having been "uncommanded," which meant that the water in the canal could not reach the designated acreage, or as having been ravaged by drought or pestilence. In fact, the unspoken assumption was that the villagers would, as a matter of course, be allowed to underreport the amount of canal water they used, and that in return they would give the *patwari*, who received only a nominal remuneration from the government, a rent-free house

and a tithe in the form of grain, vegetables, and fodder.
So the *khasra* was only a formal record, whose looks
counted for more than its substance. Its paper was extremely thin, and an entry, once made, could not be
erased or written over. One day, when Daddyji was
copying some of Lalaji's field notes into the book, he
made a mistake and tried to erase it. When Lalaji saw
the erasure, he was paralyzed with rage, so that, though
he tried, he couldn't raise his hand to strike the boy.
Then Lalaji noticed that the eraser had not gone
through the paper, and he ingeniously applied a solu-
tion of gum and ink to the spot on the page—writing
in the margin, in his beautiful Urdu script, "Ink was
spilled on this page by a little child, who did not realize
that this was the *khasra*."

Perhaps because of the ambiguous way in which
Lalaji had to earn his livelihood, he was insistent upon
his own importance. His bearing was that of a polished
courtier, and he was strong, laconic, and dictatorial. He
seldom ate with the family, and even preferred to smoke
his hookah in solitude. He scarcely ever talked to anyone at home; Daddyji remembers that in Lalaji's entire
lifetime they had at the most twenty or thirty direct
exchanges. He kept a private diary—a sort of commonplace book—in which he capped his observations and
thoughts with portentous quotations from Urdu and
Persian: "*Mushkil-e-nest ke asan nah shawad/ Mard
bayad ke hirasan nah shawad*" ("To the patient and
confident, no difficulty is difficult"); "*Kar-e-duniya/
Kase tamam na kard*" ("At journey's end, no man can
say that he has done all he started out to do"); "*Kam
insan ka insan se parta hai zaroor,/ Bat reh jati hai aur*

waqt guzar jata hai" ("Sooner or later one needs the help of another; the need is quickly forgotten, not so the help"); "*Yeh chaman yoonhi rahega aur hazaroon janwar,/ Apni apni boliyan sab bolkar ur ja yenge*" ("This garden shall ever remain, even when thousands of birds, after singing their songs, have flown away"). When he was not writing in his diary or absorbed in the intricacies of the *khasra*, he was studying a book of Unani medicine and concocting herbal powders, or reading his newspaper—a rabble-rousing Urdu paper called *Hindustan*—and delivering terse political pronouncements.

Lalaji was determined that his brothers and sons should break loose from the superstition and backwardness of village life, and leave the banyan tree and the iron skullcap for the city. He wanted them to have the education that had never been within his reach. Haru Ram, Lalaji's middle brother, showed no interest in learning, but Ganga Ram was studious, and Lalaji sent him to primary and secondary schools in various towns. When Ganga Ram finished school, however, he said to Lalaji that perhaps he should now take up a trade.

"You will become the first university graduate in the history of the family," Lalaji declared. "If you aim your arrow at the sky, it will certainly fly over the tops of the trees."

And in June, 1901, Ganga Ram graduated from Dayanand Anglo-Vernacular College, an institution in Lahore run by the Arya Samaj. As a result, the Arya Samaj—a new Hindu reform movement, founded by Swami Dayanand Saraswati—became an important force in the life of the family. The movement aimed at restoring Hinduism to its original "Aryan purity," contending that since Vedic times Hindu society had become encrusted with superstition, and so had easily fallen victim to the Muslim and British conquerors. After graduation, Ganga Ram came to stay for the summer with the family in the village of Kahangarh, where they were living at the time. Except that he always had a book in his hand, there was nothing in his manner to indicate that he was the first university graduate in the family; he still tried to walk and talk like Lalaji, and he had grown a long, thick mustache exactly like Lalaji's. All the same, everyone made no end of a fuss over him. Though he was tall and handsome, he had always been thin, and was prone to colds that lasted for months. To build him up, Lalaji now arranged for Bhabiji to serve as many chickens as the number of days of Ganga Ram's stay.

Daddyji was perpetually at Ganga Ram's heels, and every morning the little nephew would take his city uncle a repast of buttermilk and peeled almonds that Bhabiji had prepared with her own hands. Ganga Ram— or Bhaji (Older Brother) Ganga Ram, as the children called him—could be found sitting in the shade of a pipal tree outside the village gate, wearing a turban tied high on his head and stroking his mustache. As he ate and drank, he would give Daddyji lessons from the Urdu primer and teach him English words, whose exotic sounds enchanted the boy. Bhaji Ganga Ram would spend the rest of the day absorbed in his own studies, but in the evenings he would go for a walk along the canal bank, and Daddyji would tag along and, this time, get lessons in arithmetic.

By the time Daddyji was about seven years old, he had learned by heart the verses and stories in the first three Urdu primers, and could do elementary sums on a slate. He was considered old enough to attend primary school in the nearby town of Atari. Bhaji Ganga Ram, who by then had spent a year at a teachers' training college in Lahore, took him to the school for a placement examination and, for the school record, arbitrarily gave his birth date as December 25, 1895. (Thereafter it became his official birth date.) Daddyji was the first to finish, and he stood up, putting down his slate. But when the examiner looked at it, he found that the boy had got two out of five sums wrong. He was placed in the third primary class.

On the way home, Bhaji Ganga Ram stopped and slapped Daddyji across the face. "That will teach you to be hasty," he said. "Next time, be the last to finish. Revise, and make sure that you have got the right answer."

Daddyji says that he is glad he learned this lesson so early in life, but that his cheek still smarts when he thinks of it.

Daulat ram, Lalaji's third child, was a year and a half younger than Daddyji, and resembled him so closely that the brothers were often mistaken for each other, even by their own relatives. They both had thin, strong bodies, prominent Mehta noses, dark-brown eyes, and straight black hair. Daulat Ram followed Daddyji everywhere and tried to copy him in everything. Each morning, the two brothers would get up while it was

still dark and go to the village well. It was beside a bo
tree and was planted all around with carrots, radishes,
cabbages, lilac, and acacia. They would clean their teeth
with twigs, and they would bathe—Daulat Ram would
pour some water on Daddyji, and Daddyji would pour
some on him. After this, they would walk to school, a
couple of miles away along the Grand Trunk Road, the
famous old highway running across North India. Sometimes they would sit on a milestone and finish their
homework, or watch the kites and crows circling above.
Then they would continue briskly, swinging their satch-
els and their lunch bundles, which had been tenderly
packed by their older sister, Bibi Parmeshwari Devi.
There was no school for girls in the region, and Bibi
Parmeshwari Devi, an intelligent, curious child, who
helped Bhabiji around the house, took a vicarious pleasure in her brothers' achievements, sending them off to
school with a prodigious lunch of parathas (fried unleavened wheat bread), along with a special potato dish,
some scallions, some mango pickles, and, depending on
the season, a couple of bananas or oranges. The brothers
would take care that they did not accidentally come in
contact with sweepers, tanners, or any other Untouchables along the way, for Manji had given them strict
instructions to throw away the food if it should be so
defiled and to buy sweetmeats for their lunch. As an
added precaution, Manji kept a vessel of Ganga water
to purify them when they got home. But such measures
were unnecessary; the Untouchables knew their place
all too well, and kept their distance. When the brothers
reached the school, they would tie their lunch high up

on a branch of the pipal tree that stood in the school-yard, and go to their classes.

The school was a small, U-shaped red brick build-ing of three rooms—two serving as classrooms and the third as living quarters for the schoolteacher, who was the Atari *maulvi*. The pupils sat on reed mats on the packed-earth floor and were taught reading, dictation, and arithmetic—all by rote. The *maulvi* was a short, thin, wizened man with a beard and a severely clipped mustache, and he had a stern manner. He kept with him at all times a cane, moist and supple, which he would flourish when he walked. He would swat the hands or the bottom of any miscreant, and if his stu-dent monitors made a mistake, he would thwack them, too. Yet the *maulvi* lived for the most part off the pa-tronage of his charges; he would order each child to bring a couple of pounds of wheat flour and a lump of crude sugar to school whenever the district inspector of education was expected on his bimonthly visit. Osten-sibly, the supplies were for the dignitary's meals, but once the inspector had been fêted, the *maulvi* would live off the surplus until the next tour of inspection. Sometimes he would even take some of the food to his real home, in a village six miles away, where his wives and children lived. He walked there and back every second Sunday, and on the infrequent occasions when he received a salary increment he would add a new wife to his large family.

Close by the school was a big banyan tree, and next to it was an open space where the children played their version of hockey, with sticks cut from the tree and with a ball made by Bhabiji and contributed by Daddyji. The ball, a wood-and-cloth affair, was stitched all around with strong string, and inside it was a peach stone, which rattled as the ball bounced about the field.

When Daddyji was not studying, or playing hockey, he ran about the village with the other little boys, dashing between the legs of horses, cows, and buffaloes. He fed Lalaji's horse and took it to the village well for water. He gathered duck and peacock eggs from the canal bank and put them in the hen's nest; when the hen hatched the eggs, he made pets of the ducklings and peachicks. He bought myna birds and taught them to talk: *"Ram, Ram, mera nam Ganga Ram"* ("Ram, Ram, my name is Ganga Ram"). He sat for hours—sometimes until twilight—watching the village carpenter, cobbler, or oil presser at work, and playing in wood shavings or with leather scraps. He stood by the forge of the village blacksmith, wondering how something as hard and black as iron could be made so malleable and glowing.

So his life ran, from season to Punjabi season—from winter to spring to summer to the monsoon to autumn to winter again.

WHEN DADDYJI was about nine, Ganga Devi, Lalaji's youngest sister, who lived in a village near Burkhurdar with her husband, their daughter, and three sons, suddenly developed an abscess in her armpit and a fever. She took to her bed and called her husband to her side. "I have got the plague. I am going to die tomorrow,"

she said. It was during a winter of bubonic plague in which more than half a million Punjabis had already died. "Please ask all my dear ones to come in the morning. I would like to take leave of them."

In the morning, under her direction, Bahali Ram, her seven-year-old son, swept the floor between her charpoy and the wall, and plastered it with cow dung, covered one part of the plastered floor with a heavy cotton pad, and spread over that a white linen sheet.

When Lalaji, Bhabiji, Manji, Daddyji, and the other relatives arrived, Ganga Devi got down from her charpoy and sat on the sheet. She made them sit all around her on the sanctified floor and, propping herself up against the wall, opened a Hindi copy of the Gita in her lap (she had learned to read from Bhaji Ganga Ram) and read them a few verses from the scriptures:

"As the soul in this body passes through childhood, youth, and old age, so [after departure from this body] it passes on to another body. . . .

"Just as a man casts off worn-out clothes and takes on others that are new, so the embodied soul casts off worn-out bodies and takes on others that are new.

"Weapons do not cut it, nor does fire burn it; waters do not make it wet, nor does wind make it dry.

"It is uncleavable, it cannot be burnt, it can be neither wetted nor dried. It is eternal, omnipresent, unchanging, and immovable. . . .

"It is called unmanifest, unthinkable, and immutable; therefore, knowing it as such, thou shouldst not grieve."

She called her husband to her and made him promise in front of all the witnesses that he would never re-marry. She lay down on the sheet, with her head to the north, in the direction of the legendary home of her Aryan ancestors—and so the final resting place of her soul—and within a few minutes she was dead.

I I

CITY

ONE AFTERNOON, LALAJI TOOK THE ENTIRE FAMILY in a tonga from Kahangarh to Amritsar so that they might see the switching on of the first electric lights in the district. The lights had been installed several weeks earlier to illuminate the most sacred shrine of the Sikhs, the Golden Temple. The city was so thronged with villagers who had trudged miles to see the new marvel that the family had to get down from the tonga and proceed on foot. After some time, they reached the wide marble steps of the temple. They took off their shoes, washed their feet in the temple footbath, and descended to the marble terrace surrounding the sacred tank for ritual bathing. Somehow they managed to find space, and they sat down to wait until six-thirty, the hour of the illumination.

From time to time, Lalaji would take out a large pocket watch he had recently bought, consult it, and call out "Fifteen minutes to six-thirty," "Twelve minutes to six-thirty," and so on.

Daddyji kept his eyes on the big milky globes installed around the sacred tank and the gilded domes of the temple. Exactly at six-thirty, the domes were miraculously flooded with a steady incandescence.

The crowds leaped to their feet and shouted, "*Sat Sri Akal!*" ("True Timeless One!").

❦

Early one autumn morning, when the water glistened in the fresh furrows of the brown fields, Manji and three of her grandchildren boarded a slow local train at Atari for Lahore, and from there they took the Karachi Mail for the twenty-four-hour journey to Multan, on the river Chenab. Daddyji was much excited, though all he knew about the city was one Urdu couplet, which chug-chugged in his head: *"Chahar chiz ast tohfa-i Multan:/ Gard, garma, gada, o goristan"* ("Four things are the gifts of Multan: Dust, heat, beggars, and tombs").

Daddyji was ten and Daulat Ram almost nine, and both of them had gone as far as they could in the Atari primary school. They were eager to start their real education with Bhaji Ganga Ram, who, after his marriage, in 1903, had become headmaster of the Arya Samaj high school in Multan. Lalaji had long since worked out a plan whereby his sons, as they finished their local schooling, would go to Bhaji Ganga Ram in the city for their advanced education. But when Daddyji and Daulat Ram were making ready to leave, Bibi Parmeshwari Devi had clamored to go with them. On her own, she had learned to read and write Urdu and Hindi, and although the education of girls was uncommon, she longed to get at least a taste of formal schooling before she was married off—she was already thirteen. Lalaji, after some thought, had given his permission. So the three children had set off in the custody of Manji, who was herself eager to spend some time with her city son.

When their train arrived in Multan, they were met

by Bhaji Ganga Ram. Not only was he lost forever to the village but he also seemed to have acquired the wary air of a city dweller. He helped Manji into the front seat of a tonga while the children clambered on behind. The tonga-wallah flicked his whip at the dusty flanks of his horse, and soon they were riding past imposing mosques and mausoleums and winding through *gullis* amid grimy tenements, open sewers, fetid odors, and unidentifiable noises. The tonga pulled up in front of a four-story brick tenement house. "We're home," Bhaji Ganga Ram said, and he led them up a flight of stairs to three stuffy rooms looking out on an air shaft with a wooden parapet.

Every morning thereafter, Daddyji and Daulat Ram would set out from the tenement with their slates and copybooks and make their way through the crush of tongas and hawkers' carts to the Arya Samaj high school, in the sedate British cantonment outside the city wall. Here they would study English alongside the sons of the privileged Indians—high-ranking government officers, advocates, and landowners. Meanwhile, Bibi Parmeshwari Devi attended an Arya Samaj primary school for girls nearby.

Evenings at home were somewhat strained. Chhoti ("little") Bhabiji, as Bhaji Ganga Ram's wife, Upala Devi, was called, seemed sad and withdrawn. Daddyji didn't know why, but guessed that possibly it was because she had not yet had any children. Once, while he was playing on the parapet, he overheard a gossipy neighbor woman say, "If she is childless, it's her own fault. What do you expect from a cat bride?" Daddyji wanted to put a hot coal on the neighbor woman's superstitious tongue. Although Chhoti Bhabiji was very pretty—she was small and delicate, with long black hair —she had blue eyes, which, no matter how becoming, were considered to be an evil omen, because cats had blue eyes and cats brought bad luck. As a good Arya Samajist, Bhaji Ganga Ram abhorred all superstitions, and flouted even the commonest of them, such as not going out on an important errand after drinking a glass of milk or after someone had sneezed.

Daddyji discovered that where the children were concerned, Bhaji Ganga Ram was as strict a taskmaster as ever. He constantly held up to them the Arya Samaj virtues of thrift, abstinence, and industry, and expected them to measure up to his standard of moral rectitude. He made them abandon the lackadaisical ways of rustics, teaching them to clean their shoes, to look after their own clothes, and to cultivate habits of punctuality and discipline. Every Sunday morning at eight o'clock, he took the whole family to a meeting of the Arya Samaj. There the congregation chanted mantras as they threw incense and ghi into a fire, and then listened to lengthy lectures exhorting them to spurn superstition and idolatry, to study the ancient glories of Hinduism, and to emulate their Aryan forefathers.

After the children and Manji had lived with Bhaji Ganga Ram in Multan for a year or so, he moved them all to Amritsar, where he taught in a government school for another year, and where the children continued their studies. Bhaji Ganga Ram was then appointed the superintendent of Quadrangle, the boarding house of Government College, in Lahore, and he moved there with Chhoti Bhabiji, Daddyji, and Daulat Ram—Manji having returned to the village, and Bibi Parmeshwari Devi having been married, with great *éclat*, to a petty official, Mukand Lal Anand.

Ever since Daddyji could remember, he had been hearing about Lahore. Lalaji had always said that the fortunes of the family would be made there ("Aim your arrow at the sky"), and Bhaji Ganga Ram had always talked about the city as the educational center of the world. As a child, Daddyji would ask Manji to tell him about his grandfather's great journey to Lahore, and she would say, "I remember that when he came back from there he had an entire cloth shop behind his saddle. All the villagers gathered around him, and he said to them, 'Touch! Touch!' They had the hands of working people, but even they could tell that the cloth from Lahore was softer than melted butter." And now Daddyji had actually come to live in Lahore, the clamorous, clangorous city. Here there were whole streets of cobblers, weavers, and potters, and there was an entire bazaar for every imaginable trade—one for metalworkers, one for carpetmakers, one for dyers, one for cloth merchants, one for dry grocers, one for goldsmiths and silversmiths, one for confectioners, one for savory cooks. There was even a whole city-within-a-city of courtesans, called Hira Mandi ("gem market"), which was dead and deserted by day but by night was glittering and alive with the sound of music and laughter. Behind the bazaars and lanes were rabbit warrens of *mohallas*, or blocks of tenement houses, opening onto squares that were entered by still narrower *gullis*, and these *mohallas* and *gullis* contained more life and variety than could be found in any village. Bhaji Ganga Ram, however, had taken lodgings in a new, open part of the city, where the British government officers and the Indians attached to the British establishment lived. These lodgings—three rooms and a kitchen, one flight up—were somewhat better than the ones in Multan. But what Daddyji liked most of all about them was a discovery he made within minutes of reaching them. Just outside the building was a curved pipe sticking up out of the ground, with a handle on top. When the handle was raised and lowered, water came gushing out of the mouth of the pipe, which was high enough to sit under. Daddyji had never seen anything like it, and the first thing he did in Lahore was to take a bath.

After they had been in Lahore a few weeks, Daddyji noticed that Bhaji Ganga Ram was becoming increasingly irritable. Perhaps his new duties were too taxing; he was required to spend the night in his room at Quadrangle, and he had to walk home for all his meals, which he ate in total silence. Perhaps the fact that he and Chhoti Bhabiji had not yet succeeded in having a child—Chhoti Bhabiji had suffered several miscarriages and stillbirths—had begun to tell on him, especially since Lalaji and Bhabiji by now had a family of six, five of whom were sons. Perhaps a new enthusiasm of Daddyji's was getting on his nerves. Daddyji and Daulat Ram had been entered in Central Model School, whose headmaster—an Englishman, Mr. Tydeman—was fond of quoting *"Mens sana in corpore sano"* and had made hockey and cricket part of the school curriculum. Sports were in Daddyji's blood, and once he had come under the aegis of Mr. Tydeman he never missed a chance to play either. Daddyji would march about in his khaki shorts and his white shirt with its starched collar, brandishing his hockey stick. Bhaji Ganga Ram, however, considered all sports a waste of time, a luxury for the idle rich, an affectation of Anglicized Indians. At the Arya Samaj school he had attended, the students had been pious, austere, and upright, and had dressed simply in the traditional loose pajamas and shirts. Indeed, Chhoti Bhabiji's nephew Gian Chand, who had just arrived at Bhaji Ganga Ram's for his education and was going to that Arya Samaj school, became a pet of Bhaji Ganga Ram's. He was frail, studious, and easily influenced—a paragon of all the virtues that Daddyji and Daulat Ram lacked. Often, when the three boys sat down at home and boasted about what they had done in their schools, Bhaji Ganga Ram would nod knowingly and observe, "*Kheloge kudoge hoge kharab,/ Parhoge likhoge banoge nawab*" ("If you play and jump about, you will become a no-good; if you read and write, you will become a potentate").

During the long summer vacation the year before Daddyji's graduation from Central Model School, Lalaji put two hundred rupees in Daddyji's hand and sent him off to Pattoki. Pattoki was one of a number of new planned communities southwest of Lahore that the government was then developing as part of the Bari Doab Canal irrigation project. It was the first time that Daddyji, who was then about fourteen, had been anywhere on his own, and he was intoxicated with his mission, which was to oversee the improvement of a house, the family's first piece of urban property.

The house had a tangled history. It happened that Lalaji's oldest sister, Dayavanti, was married to Haveli Ram, a rich moneylender who lived in Amritsar. Several years earlier, Haveli Ram had written to Lalaji suggesting that the two brothers-in-law buy contiguous plots of land in Pattoki and build family houses side by side. He said that the price of land in the new urban communities was going up rapidly, and, since Lalaji had little ready cash, offered to lend him the necessary money. Lalaji was tempted by the prospect of a new house in a modern town, for there was no going back to the ancestral village. His brother Haru Ram, who had been left custodian of the family property in Nawankote, had proved to be neither a good shopkeeper nor a good farmer; pilfering of merchandise from the shop had become so common that he had been forced to close it down, and he had fared no better with the family land left under his care. He had quarrelled with his first cousins, who lived in the same compound and shared a private well with him. They had threatened to break his head. Lalaji had visited Nawankote and settled the quarrel, but his last bond with the village had been loosened. He therefore gladly assented to Haveli Ram's proposal, even entrusting the building of his own house to his brother-in-law. Haveli Ram and Lalaji had agreed that the two houses would be identical, but when Lalaji went to Pattoki after a few months to see how his house was coming along, he was shocked to find that although the two houses were the same in design—they had to conform to a standard development plan—Haveli Ram's was built with good bricks and the best grade of cement, and showed superior workmanship,

while Lalaji's was shoddy and insubstantial-looking.
The only explanation he could think of was that Haveli
Ram wanted to publicize the difference in their worldly
positions. Lalaji went over to Haveli Ram's house,
where Haveli Ram was now living, and charged him
with a breach of their agreement. Haveli Ram replied
by asking for immediate repayment of his loan, and
he demanded much more money than he could con-
ceivably have spent on the house. Although Haveli Ram
was so notorious as a moneylender that he was afraid
to go about alone at night, Lalaji had never imagined
that a man would exploit his own brother-in-law. When
Lalaji protested that he had no money, Haveli Ram
said, "In that case, Brother-in-Law, I have no choice but
to attach your house and land in payment of my loan."
In the short time since the land was bought, however,
it had increased in value many times over, and Lalaji
couldn't think of parting with it. He said as much to
Haveli Ram, who thereupon brought suit against Lalaji
for defaulting on the loan. After two years' litigation,
the court appointed an arbitrator to settle the dispute,
and he decided in favor of Haveli Ram. (It was said
that the arbitrator had been bribed.) Lalaji somehow
raised the money for the repayment of both the principal and the interest, however, and was allowed to keep
the house and land.

So it was that Daddyji now found himself in Pattoki, remodelling the house. He hired laborers, super-
vised them, paid them with money that Lalaji sent him
regularly, and ordered whatever he liked to eat at the
local *tandur*. (Lalaji had admonished Daddyji to keep
his distance from Haveli Ram and his family.) Alto-

gether, he spent a couple of very happy months in Pattoki, though his pleasure was tinged with bitterness whenever he looked over the wall common to the two houses, for there he would see Dayavanti lying on a charpoy in her courtyard, loaded with gold ornaments from head to toe. She had grown very heavy and bulky, and it was clearly an effort for her to bestir herself. She was on the charpoy more or less continuously from morning to evening, wrapped in her best finery, commanding her servants, taking her meals, fanning herself, and dozing.

After finishing the house in Pattoki, Daddyji returned to Lahore to find that Bhaji Ganga Ram's household had been increased by the arrival of Balwant, Lalaji's third son, and of Jaswant, Haru Ram's son, both of whom had finished their primary schooling and had been sent as a matter of course to Bhaji Ganga Ram for their further education.

DADDYJI PASSED his final, matriculation examination in the first division. Lalaji came to Lahore to discuss Daddyji's future, and there was a meeting in Bhaji Ganga Ram's office in Quadrangle. Bhaji Ganga Ram sat in his usual armchair, behind his desk; Lalaji reclined on a cane sofa; and Daddyji stood at a respectful distance.

"I've put Gian Chand down for engineering school, Lalaji," Bhaji Ganga Ram said. "I would advise you to send him"—he pointed to Daddyji—"to a professional school, too. There is no better course for boys from good middle-class families like ours than to acquire a profession—engineering, law, or medicine—and then enter government service and rise by hard, honest work."

"I don't think he should be pushed into a career yet," Lalaji said. "He should go to Government College and get a general education first."

Daddyji scarcely dared to look pleased—Government College was where he wanted to go.

Neither man liked his opinions to be questioned, and there was a long silence, during which Lalaji lit a cigarette and drew on it. (When he didn't have his hookah, he smoked a brand of cigarettes called Scissors.)

"Government College!" Bhaji Ganga Ram said at last. "He'll only fritter away his time on hockey and cricket, and ape the British sahibs, like other Quadrangle boarders. Next, he'll want to be a maharaja!"

Lalaji blew out a thin plume of smoke and said, "Are we, then, to be less than maharajas?"

III

COLLEGE

D ADDYJI FELT HE HAD BEEN TAPPED BY DESTINY. IT was the first day of his first term at Government College. He walked along the oval Government College driveway encircling the hockey field and went up to the main building, a large Gothic structure. The monsoon had just ended, and the oval field was flooded, so that the façade was reflected in the water, acquiring an aspect of majesty. Here and there were students in twos and threes, strolling about and chatting. Daddyji went along the open veranda, which ran around the sides and the back of the building. Clearly, the buildings and grounds of Government College could have no rival, he thought. Beyond the back veranda were grass tennis courts, and beyond them was the principal's house. To one side of the main building were Quadrangle, the football field, and the bungalows of professors, many of whom were Oxonians or Cantabrigians. Eventually, he went inside the building—into a large hall. He walked over to a table and began filling out his course-application form. While he was writing down his birth date, he became aware that someone was looking over his shoulder.

"My dear Mehta," boomed an English voice. "Do you realize you were born on the birthday of Our Lord?"

Daddyji turned and looked the Englishman straight in the eye. "No," he said. "I have never given much thought to when I was born."

The Englishman laughed, and introduced himself

as Professor Gerard Wathen. "You certainly look like a sportsman. What games do you play?"

"Hockey and cricket, sir."

Professor Wathen explained that the college was divided up into a number of small student groups that competed in sports, and that his group and the one headed by Professor Jones were the two that were most highly regarded. "I want you in my group," he said, and he initialled Daddyji's form with a "G. W."

During Daddyji's first term, Government College was astir with the news that an "America-returned" swami had come to Lahore and was camped on the banks of the Ravi, three miles away. He lectured every afternoon, and one Sunday, after tiffin, Daddyji and some of his classmates went out to hear him. The swami was a short, dark Bengali, dressed in a saffron-colored robe and wearing gold earrings, and as they sat around him on the bare ground, he spoke to them in an excited falsetto, now and again shaking his head and making the earrings swing hypnotically.

"We Indians have got used to bemoaning our fate," he said. "We sit back on our haunches in our hovels, living off our relatives, who throw food to us as they would to a dog, out of false family obligation. Cut your ties and strike out for the Land of the Free—the United States of America." He stretched out an arm beckoningly, displacing the ample folds of his robe. "In the New World, there is dignity of labor, and men of all castes and creeds can earn lots of money. There, everyone works with his hands and no one is derided for it. In God's own country, land is so abundant that it is being distributed free of cost to all comers. There is enough for everybody, and I prophesy that the United States will leave the British and the British Empire far behind. In the Land of Plenty, all men have opportunity."

Throughout the lecture, the swami appeared to be staring at Daddyji, as if he were speaking solely for Daddyji's benefit—as if he were saying, "You, too, can embark for the Promised Land." Daddyji was about sixteen. He was gregarious, energetic, and good-looking, and made friends easily. His prowess on the playing fields had already made him an object of adulation. He felt he was mature and able to think for himself. After all, he had lived away from his parents for six years, under the unrelenting scrutiny of Bhaji Ganga Ram, whom he regarded as temperamentally antipathetic. His mission at Pattoki and his entrance into Government College had filled him with self-confidence. He fancied that adventure was in his character, and he went away from the lecture saying to himself, "Nothing ventured, nothing gained."

A few days later, Daddyji went home to the village to visit Lalaji and Bhabiji; Manji had died, at the age of eighty, having remained clear-headed to the last. There Daddyji witnessed a scene that still haunts him. Because Bhabiji had been guilty of some trifling oversight (Daddyji has never been able to recall what it was), Lalaji went into a rage, like a horse with the devil astride. He started shouting at Bhabiji, heaping curses on her and her ancestors, calling her every foul name in the language. She sat with her head bent over a pot of lentils she was cooking for his dinner; she was crying silently. He must have railed at her for an

hour. Long before Lalaji's rage had been curbed, Daddyji decided that he would never again sleep under his
father's roof. Bhaji Ganga Ram and Lalaji were two
of a kind, he told himself, and he would have to rescue
his mother. He would terminate his studies, run away
to Bombay, enlist as a deckhand on a ship, and sail
west. He would get a job in America, and then he
would send for his mother and brothers.

What he did next he didn't divulge to any of his
children until he was in his early seventies, in case a
child of his should follow his bad example.

He rolled up his bedding and, carrying it on his
back, stole away. A third-class ticket from Lahore to
Bombay, a thousand miles and forty-three hours away on
the Frontier Mail, was twelve rupees; Daddyji had eighteen rupees all told, but when he arrived at the Lahore
station he found it so crowded that he couldn't even get
near the ticket window. As it happened, the next day
was the twelfth of December, 1911, and King George V
was holding his Coronation Durbar in Delhi that day
to inaugurate the city as the new capital of Imperial
India. All of Lahore seemed bound for the Durbar to
catch a glimpse of the Emperor. The crush was so thick
that Daddyji was swept along to the train, which was
itself so crowded that people were hanging out of the
windows and clinging to the footboards and sitting on
top of the carriages. Somehow, he managed to push
his way into a third-class compartment and wedge himself between a couple of bedrolls on the luggage rack.
Eventually, the train pulled out of the station, and he
was on his way to Bombay.

At Delhi station, he was unable to get down to buy

his ticket; the crowds there were, if anything, denser than those in Lahore. The arrangements for the Durbar were so strict that most of the people who had come to Delhi were being turned away and were now trying to get out of the city. Daddyji wasn't able to buy a ticket until the train reached the junction station of Itarsi, where he was required to pay only the fare from there to Bombay, which was four rupees. He thus reached his destination, the next morning, with fourteen rupees in his pocket. The cavernous Bombay station hummed with humanity, and people jostled one another as if they were at a village fair. He walked out onto the street wondering where in all this crushing vastness he would find a little space to spread out his meagre bedding. He saw a row of victorias waiting for fares. He shared a victoria with a stranger in a dhoti, and got himself dropped off at the nearest *dharamshala* (pilgrims' hostel). It consisted of a couple of rooms with concrete floors, and it had a veranda, and a courtyard that was open to the sky. The *dharamshala* was next to a shabby temple, and people were constantly coming and going, but the place was neat and clean. He took possession of a corner of the veranda by spreading out his bedding there, and then went out.

He plunged into the maelstrom of the city, and after a great deal of walking he found his way to the offices of Mackinnon, Mackenzie & Co., agents for the Peninsular & Oriental Steam Navigation Co. The clerk in the outer office took one look at him, made a snide remark about his boyish appearance (he was dressed in a shirt and khaki shorts), scolded him for playing truant from school, and shooed him away. He made his way to the offices of the *Times of India*, where copies of that morning's edition were displayed and could be read free of charge. He scanned the advertisement notices for a "Wanted—Matriculation Passed," but in vain. He went to the Post and Telegraph Office, which was nearby, and inquired about vacancies for a postal clerk. There were none. He wandered along the seafront and spent the afternoon watching people taking the air or playing football. He longed to join in the game, but realized that to the players he was a mere street urchin—perhaps a piece of the human flotsam regularly cast up from other parts of India on the Bombay shore. He returned to his corner of the veranda and lay down, and willed himself to dream about the swami's Land of Opportunity.

His first day set the pattern for his subsequent days. He would first visit the grand offices of venerable shipping companies, of newspapers, and of government agencies, and then he would take the sea air, sometimes walking about with his hands in his pockets and sometimes sitting listlessly on the parapet above the sea, getting sprayed by the waves. He subsisted almost entirely on *hari chhals* (green bananas), which were sold on street corners, three for a pice. They were sweet, but they sat in his stomach like bullets.

One evening, when he had been in Bombay for a week, he returned to the *dharamshala* from his day's wanderings to find that it had a new resident—a sadhu with a long black beard and the horizontal stripes of an orthodox Hindu on his forehead. He was dressed in clean white clothes and had a wide piece of ochre-colored cloth wrapped around his shoulders; he was sitting cross-legged on the veranda with an image of Lord Krishna in front of him, and was holding a meeting.

Daddyji joined the audience and engaged the sadhu in a debate about idolatry; as an Arya Samajist, Daddyji had heard many discourses on the subject and abhorred idol worship in any form.

After the meeting, the sadhu called Daddyji to him. "So wise, and yet so small," he said. "And also so wrong. I shall make you my chela."

"I am the captain of my fate and the master of my soul," Daddyji said. "I have no intention of becoming anyone's chela."

"You will learn better," the sadhu said. He arranged with a rich sweetmeat vender who was in the audience to give Daddyji four annas' worth of sweetmeats free every day.

Daddyji accepted the arrangement, making no secret of the fact that it was a mere convenience, which was to last only until he could shake the dust of India from his feet.

When Daddyji had been in Bombay for three weeks, he saw a notice outside the office of the magistrate of Bombay Presidency listing a vacancy for an Urdu-English translator. He went in and applied, and, along with several other candidates, was given an examination for the position. They were asked to write a translation exercise and an English essay on either "The Benefits of Music" or "The Blessings of the Raj." As it happened, music had been an essay subject on Daddyji's matriculation-examination paper, and he had written on it with distinction. He now repeated his earlier performance, holding forth on the seductive tones of the snake charmer's pipe and the voluptuous melody of Lord Krishna's flute, which so thrilled the cows and milkmaids who heard it that they followed him to the ends of the earth. Daddyji was declared first in the examination for translator and was called in for an interview with the Presidency magistrate.

He was led into a big room with a dais at one end. On the dais was a big desk, and sitting behind it, in a big chair, was a big Englishman. Daddyji waited at the foot of the dais, and the Englishman looked down at him, evidently surprised at finding the applicant to be such a small boy.

"Come on up, my boy, up next to me," he thundered, and he added kindly, "Don't be afraid."

Daddyji did as he was told, and rested his hands on the desk for support. The magistrate complimented him on his fine penmanship and on his knowledge of Urdu and English grammar.

Daddyji flushed with excitement; he was certain he had been selected for the post.

"Why aren't you in school?" the magistrate demanded.

"Sir, I am in college," Daddyji said, drawing himself up.

"What say? College? What college? What is its name? Where is it?"

Daddyji recognized the trap. "I prefer not to say."

"My boy, where do you live? What is your address?"

"I'm putting up in a *dharamshala*," Daddyji said.

"There are dozens of *dharamshalas*—nay, hundreds —in Bombay! Where is your *dharamshala*?"

"I prefer not to say."

The magistrate became thoughtful, and after a while he asked, "How much money do you have on you?"

Daddyji became aware that hot tears were falling on his hands. Sometime that morning—he wasn't quite sure when or where—someone had stolen his last rupee.

"Come on, boy, make a clean breast of it."

Daddyji remained silent, and the magistrate, assuming a commanding, harsh tone, said, "I can find out your address without stirring from this chair, but it will be better for you if you tell me yourself."

When Daddyji still didn't speak, the magistrate called in a police officer. "Get this boy's address from his application form," he ordered. "Find out everything about him."

Daddyji felt that he had met his Waterloo. He blurted everything out.

The magistrate heard his story and then asked him whether he would prefer to return to Lahore voluntarily or under police escort.

Daddyji had scarcely enough money for a *hari chhal*—how could he pay the fare back to Lahore? But now he heard the magistrate telling him that the government would bear the expense of his return, and he yielded graciously.

The magistrate deputed the police officer to accompany Daddyji to the *dharamshala* while he got his belongings, and to put him on the train, and before the

evening was out he was on the Frontier Mail, this time
in an empty second-class compartment, whose seats,
unlike those in third class, were cushioned. To his surprise, he felt glad to be going back to Lahore, for the
day before his encounter with the magistrate, while
looking for a job, he had met a businessman and philan-
thropist, who, like the magistrate, had extracted from
him the story of his plight and had counselled him to
go back. He had also given Daddyji a letter of introduction to a friend who lived in a big house in Lahore
and could take Daddyji in, so that he would never have
to go back and face the conditions he had run away
from. And now, as he looked out of the window and
saw the warm, rich brown earth in the gathering dusk,
he felt that, after all, this Indian land was his own—that
he belonged to the soil from which he had sprung. He
remembered the thrill he had experienced hearing the
nationalist speeches of the Arya Samajists. He could
never really love another country as much as he loved
his own. He recited to himself a few lines of a poem
he had learned for his matriculation examination:

> Breathes there the man, with soul so dead,
> Who never to himself hath said,
>   This is my own, my native land!
> Whose heart hath ne'er within him burn'd,
> As home his footsteps he hath turn'd
>   From wandering on a foreign strand!

DADDYJI SPENT his first night in Lahore in the house
of the businessman's friend. The following day was
Sunday, and there was a cricket match on the Govern-

ment College grounds. He went to it and was surrounded by his classmates. They shook his hand, they
embraced him, they patted him on the back, they paraded him about the grounds. They were curious about
every detail of his adventure. They told him that his
family had been distracted by his mysterious disappear-
ance. Lalaji and Bhabiji had come to Lahore and had
published his picture in the local paper. Bhabiji had
wept for two days. Bhaji Ganga Ram had complained
bitterly at having nurtured such an ingrate. Lalaji,
while showing no outward emotion, had been heard
to say that his son and heir had been kidnapped by
Afrikaners and taken to the Transvaal to work as an
indentured servant—something that did sometimes happen. The inner circle of Daddyji's friends, who knew
about the swami, had believed that Daddyji was steam-
ing toward America and that one day he would return
as a rich Yankee.

Within an hour, Bhaji Ganga Ram heard that
Daddyji had been seen at the cricket match, and soon
Daddyji was back at Bhaji Ganga Ram's. Lalaji happened to be out, but Bhaji Ganga Ram reviled Daddyji
for being headstrong and thoughtless and feckless and
reckless and heartless. Daddyji bore up as best he could
under the onslaught, saying to himself that every cloud
has a silver lining—that during his stay in Bombay he
had learned at first hand the meaning of deprivation
and poverty, and was a wiser man for the experience.
He thought of himself as a cool-eyed, calculating gambler who knew how to run great risks for greater gains.
The passing of the years, he thought, would bring him
maturity but no regret for his actions, though he would

never go away again without first being certain that he was able to earn his livelihood.

When Lalaji returned to the house, Bhaji Ganga Ram told him at some length that he would no longer keep Daddyji under his roof or be responsible for his conduct.

Such a declaration threatened to rend the fabric of the family, but Lalaji only nodded and, without as much as a word or a glance at Daddyji, started down the stairs.

Daddyji followed him.

Without turning around, Lalaji said, "You'd better go and board at the hostel."

Daddyji, knowing the financial burden that this would place on Lalaji, said to his back, which was straight, as always, "Please do not worry about me. I will make up with Bhaji Ganga Ram and adjust to everyone's satisfaction."

Lalaji walked away. Daddyji continued to live with Bhaji Ganga Ram, eating what little food was thereafter served him and enduring the upbraiding of his guardian.

DADDYJI COULD NEVER RESIST a test. When he had been at Government College for two years, his best friend, Gautam Kumar, who had decided on medicine as a career, sat for an examination in organic chemistry—a requirement for entrance to the King Edward Medical College. Although Daddyji had all along intended to become an engineer, he took the examination, too, just to see how high he could score. When the results were

Daddyji, College, 1912

announced, he was astonished to learn that out of a hundred and fifty students only twenty had passed and he and Gautam Kumar were two of the twenty. Daddyji felt that since those few who qualified as doctors would be eligible for the highest-paying jobs in the Punjab, it would be foolish for him not to take advantage of this piece of luck. Moreover, he had heard Lalaji express the hope that one of his sons would become a doctor. And so he decided to take up medicine.

King Edward Medical College had a large hospital attached to it, and buildings and grounds almost as impressive as those of Government College. On his first day there, Daddyji automatically named Gautam Kumar, who had been a classmate of his since his Central Model School days, as his laboratory partner, but when he looked at the class roster he saw that Gautam Kumar had chosen as his partner a new student from Delhi with whom he had become friendly. Daddyji felt betrayed, humiliated, abandoned. The very thought of the dissection hall, with its rows of cadavers and its reek of formaldehyde, nauseated him. Anyway, he preferred sports and games to studies, and he resolved that from that day on he would stay away from lectures and books and loaf his way through medical college.

That winter, the university introduced a bicycle race as an event in its winter-sports tournament, and Daddyji decided to enter it. Although bicycles were still a luxury, he was lucky enough to have wangled one from Lalaji. To get himself in trim, he started going on long bicycle treks with a class-fellow named Sukhdev, who, next to Daddyji, was the best cyclist in the university. Sometimes they would cover the seventy miles to Amritsar and back in a single day. Daddyji and Sukhdev, who was also to race in the tournament, had become such good friends that they made a pact: they would reach the finish line together and share the first prize.

In the tournament, almost from the very first, Sukhdev and Daddyji left all the other competitors behind, and, as they had planned, they freewheeled shoulder to shoulder nearly to the finish line. When they were just a few yards away, and Daddyji was already imagining how they would go up together to His Excellency the Governor of the Punjab—seated in the stands—to receive their first prize, Sukhdev suddenly put on an extra burst of speed and shot ahead. He won.

The betrayals by Gautam Kumar and Sukhdev were the first of a long series. Each time, Daddyji felt he had been cruelly duped, and yet, he says, he never succeeded in learning the ways of the wary and the cunning but continued to believe that "trust begets trust, mistrust begets mistrust." Although for a time a perfidious act would sadden him, remembering it in later years would always fill him with laughter at his gullibility. In any case, the bicycle race only whetted his appetite for competition.

In the spring, he joined a group called the Early Birds, who got up at five o'clock in the morning to practice running. One afternoon, he was sitting under a tree in Lawrence Gardens engrossed in a book; it was Holi, and he was nonchalantly dressed in a white bush shirt and a pair of white trousers that had been streaked with colored water by merrymakers. Suddenly, he was hailed by another Early Bird, Pran Nath Sondhi, who was on a bicycle and had braked at the edge of the footpath. He was jauntily dressed in a well-pressed Government College blazer—red, with gold trim and the college insignia—and red knickers, and had a pair of spiked track shoes dangling from the handlebars of his bicycle.

"I'm off to a half-mile race at Chiefs' College—it's open to all comers," he said, and he asked Daddyji if he'd like to enter the race, casually remarking that since he himself was the university champion for that year, Daddyji could hope to come in only second, at best.

Daddyji, who had injured his foot playing hockey, had been unable to compete in university track for a year, and felt that if it were not for the injury *he* would have been university champion. He had recovered, however, and now he jumped up, tied his books to the back of his bicycle, which was lying nearby, and said, "We'll see who comes in second, Sondhi."

He sped to Chiefs' College with Sondhi, threw down his bicycle, elbowed his way through the crowds to the track, and flung off his shoes for the race. One of his medical-college professors accosted him and chided him for his stained trousers and dirty bare feet, saying that no less a person than His Excellency the Governor of the Punjab was in the stands and was going to give out the prizes. Daddyji hastily told of his meeting with Sondhi, apologized, and dashed off to the starting line. The other contestants were strapping Sikhs and fierce-looking Pathans, and he feared that neither he nor Sondhi stood a chance.

At the start, the Sikhs and the Pathans pulled ahead and took a decisive lead, but Daddyji and Sondhi ran steadily. A bell rang, signalling the end of the first lap and the beginning of the second. The Sikhs and the Pathans, hearing it, thought that the race was over, and stopped. The man in the lead, a Sikh, threw up his arms and cried out, "I have won! I have won!"

The spectators began shouting, "Run, run, you fools!" But Daddyji and Sondhi had passed them by that time, and their competitors were never able to catch up.

Sondhi took the lead, but Daddyji stayed close behind and conserved his energy. In the last hundred yards, he increased his speed, eased ahead of Sondhi, and stayed ahead until he had thrown his body across the winning tape. He won the race by two yards. He heard his named called by the Governor and went up to receive the first prize, a pocket watch worth fifty rupees.

Before the day was out, he had given the watch to Bibi Parmeshwari Devi's husband and had sent a note to Sondhi saying, "It's not whether you win or lose but how you play the game that counts."

Because of his fun and games, Daddyji just missed passing his first-year medical-college examination. Neither Bhaji Ganga Ram nor Lalaji said anything to him about it. Daulat Ram, who followed his older brother into medical college, and Daddyji were to keep the fact of his failure a secret from everybody else for nearly fifty years, so that Daddyji would serve as a good example to his younger brothers and, later, to all the Mehta children.

THE SUMMER Daddyji was nineteen, he went on a six-week trek on foot through the Himalayas, amid forests of pine and deodar, past torrential waterfalls and sheer cliffs, and over slopes covered with mountain flowers and berry bushes. During the trek, he stopped at a village called Jawalamukhi. This village is renowned in the surrounding hills for a perpetual flame, which is fed by natural gas issuing from a crevice in the rock, and which is believed to be a manifestation of a goddess. A temple had been raised to the goddess on the rock, and in earlier times she had been offered human sacrifice. While Daddyji was visiting the temple, he saw a ragged pilgrim run up to the flame and cry, "O Goddess! I took *bhang* and blasphemed my guru!" (*Bhang* is a hemp intoxicant.) He drew a knife, cut off a piece of his tongue, and flung it into the flame.

Daddyji rushed to the pilgrim's side, attended to him as best he could, and then led him to a first-aid station in a ramshackle hut nearby.

While the doctor in charge, a friendly old man, was ministering to the pilgrim, a woman came in, dragging a boy of about six and a girl of about twelve. The woman and the boy looked plump and well fed, but the girl seemed emaciated, and her cheeks had a feverish flush. She had a beautiful oval face with a delicate, small nose and large, shiny greenish-blue eyes; thick golden hair loosely braided in a heavy plait hung down to her hips. She was from the hills, but she might have been from another continent. When she became aware that Daddyji was staring at her, she lowered her head and started twisting her plait.

The doctor gave her a cursory examination, and

then said to Daddyji, "Young man, would you look her over? It seems to me a simple case of influenza." He turned back to the pilgrim.

After Daddyji had examined her and taken her medical history, he concluded that she was suffering from chronic malaria and malnutrition. He gave the woman quinine and iron for her daughter, and told her to see that the girl got more to eat.

"Eat! Eat what?" the woman said, and she left abruptly with her children.

Daddyji was unable to get the girl out of his mind, and that evening, after making some inquiries about her and her family, he climbed a hill and crossed a rocky pasture to their hut; at one side of it was a pen, into which the girl and a dog were just then herding some sheep, and in the hut, as Daddyji could see from the doorway, were piled bundles of fleece, which sent out a rank odor.

Daddyji squatted down a little distance from the door, and the man of the house came out to talk with him. In a short time, Daddyji found out that the man was a shepherd, that the woman, his second wife, was the stepmother of the girl and the mother of the boy, that she took his daughter's share of the food and gave it to their son, and that she beat the girl if she complained. The shepherd was devoted to his daughter and had decided to rescue her by selling her into the harem of his employer, a raja, who owned practically everything in the area.

Daddyji was horrified, and made the shepherd promise that he would not sell her. "I will return to Jawalamukhi one day as a full-fledged doctor and personally train your daughter to be a nurse," he said, and although he never saw the girl again, he was never afterward able to think of medicine in a cold, scientific light, detached from the people it was supposed to help. He went on to stand second—or sometimes first—in his class and to win academic medals and scholarships at the Medical College.

IV

ENGLAND

O N THE THIRTEENTH DAY OF APRIL IN 1919, BRIGA-
dier General Reginald Dyer blocked the main
entrance to the Jallianwala Bagh, a park in
Amritsar, where an illegal but informal political meeting was in progress, and, without warn-
ing, ordered his troops to fire on the trapped
crowd. By the time their ammunition was exhausted,
at least three hundred and seventy-nine Indians had
been killed and twelve hundred wounded. Civil dis-
turbances followed throughout the Punjab, including
a strike by the students of all colleges. Martial law was
proclaimed, and under its decree the students of King
Edward Medical College, though they were not com-
pelled to attend classes, became virtual outlaws who had
to report for roll call at the college three times a day—
in the morning, at midday, and in the late afternoon—
on pain of being arrested or flogged. On the first day
of the roll calls, Daddyji, who was a fourth-year scholarship student and one of the leaders of the strike, was
summoned to the office of the principal of the Medical
College, Lieutenant-Colonel David Waters Sutherland.
After observing that Daddyji was one of his favorite
students, Colonel Sutherland asked him to honor the
pledge required of all scholarship holders that they
would not take part in any political activity, and pressed
Daddyji to lead the other scholarship holders back to
class. Daddyji refused on both counts. Soon after this,
the roll calls were turned into a truly harrowing ordeal.
Three times a day, the roll was called both on the col-

lege grounds and at a building three miles away, and the strikers were made to march in formation from one place to the other—a total of eighteen miles. The marches, which continued through the punishing heat of April and May, broke the strike. Late in May, the students returned to their classes, and Daddyji and the other scholarship students were rusticated.

Daddyji resolved to go to England to finish his medical education, even if he had to swim to get there. He went to the office of the deputy commissioner of Lahore, whose recommendation, along with that of the local superintendent of police, was necessary for a passport. Even though Daddyji knew that in the eyes of the government he was a dangerous insurgent, he presented his case to the officer, arguing that he was an innocent partisan of justice, and that, in any event, his activities shouldn't stand in the way of his further education.

He was prepared for summary dismissal, but the deputy commissioner, who turned out to be a member of a family well known in the Indian Civil Service for enlightened administration, said, "I agree with you."

Emboldened, Daddyji asked, "But what if the superintendent of police doesn't agree with *us*?"

The deputy commissioner picked up the telephone and spoke directly to the superintendent of police, and within a few days Daddyji had his passport.

A SECOND-CLASS passage from Bombay to London in 1920 cost eight hundred rupees. Daddyji had somehow managed to husband all his scholarship stipend for two years, which, along with his savings from what Lalaji gave him for his college expenses, amounted to nine hundred rupees. In preparation for going to England, he also borrowed five hundred rupees from a wealthy student he had coached through the medical finals. This, he hoped, would be enough to see him through an academic year in England. For postgraduate study at an English university, however, Daddyji needed a testimonial from Colonel Sutherland, who had been cool to him ever since the strike—even though the government had eventually reinstated almost all the rusticated scholarship students, and Daddyji had been able to take his medical degree after all. Through some detective work after the end of the college year, he discovered that Colonel Sutherland was vacationing at Simla, in the Punjab Himalayas.

Daddyji arrived in Simla one evening after a long journey, which had included an eight-hour tonga ride through pine and rhododendron woods, up steep slopes, and around hairpin turns. He put up in the native bazaar, and early the next day, which was bright and chilly, he climbed up to the Ridge, where Europeans out on their morning rounds were hailing one another from their rickshaws and chatting as they met on the Mall. Daddyji, watching the people go in and out of the Cecil Hotel, felt that he was already in England. Having quickly worked out a strategy for arranging a seemingly chance encounter with Colonel Sutherland, he strolled up and down in front of the Mall windows of the hotel as if he were taking a constitutional. Eventually, he spied the Colonel going into the dining room for breakfast, and briskly stepped into the hotel, where he posted himself behind the dining-room door, well out of sight. As Colonel Sutherland came out, Daddyji materialized and greeted him with a wide smile of surprised recognition.

"Hello!" said the Colonel, taken aback. "You're here celebrating your success in the finals? My heartiest congratulations!" He was in riding coat, breeches, and boots, and looked more like a country squire than like the principal of a distinguished Indian medical college.

Daddyji thanked him, and at once asked him for the testimonial. The Colonel took Daddyji to his room, and sat him down in a substantial chair in front of a fire while he wrote out a long and complimentary letter.

Back in Lahore, Daddyji was asked to dinner by an England-returned professor of his, G. D. Sondhi. (As a student, Daddyji had attended him when he was in the hospital for an abdominal operation.) Professor Sondhi, in the sanctuary of his Victorian drawing room, lectured Daddyji on the importance of cultivating good British habits. "Don't do what most Indians do, and arrive in London with a huge bedroll, a chest of spices, and a leaky tin of ghi," Professor Sondhi said. "All you need take is a toothbrush and a Dhariwal woollen blanket, as a precaution. Wherever you stay, you will be given soap, towels, bedding, and food." The Professor took Daddyji into the dining room, invited him to sit down at a long table, and served him a plate of fried fish, boiled potatoes, and garden peas. When Daddyji tried to pick up his piece of fish with a spoon, Professor Sondhi placed a fish knife and fork in Daddyji's hands and showed him how to cut the fish and how to lift it with his fork to his mouth. "Whenever you're in doubt, just watch an Englishman and copy him," Professor Sondhi said. "But don't ever speak to an Englishman until you're introduced, and always address Englishmen of good breeding as 'sir,' and never discuss age, religion, or death."

A few days later, with the feverish heat of the Punjabi summer pressing against the brain, the entire family—by now Lalaji and Bhabiji had seven children, six of whom were sons—gathered at the railway station in Lahore to see Daddyji off on the same Frontier Mail that had carried him to Bombay nine years before. They encircled him. They garlanded him. The younger brothers fought with one another over who should carry his luggage—one folded Dhariwal blanket and a small steel trunk. He scarcely heard them, and he saw them all in a blur, as if in a shadowy group photograph.

"You will see," Bhaji Ganga Ram said, shaking his head. "He'll come back with a cigar in his mouth and a missy sahib on his arm. And he'll be drinking whiskey instead of milk. All England-returned are the same."

"Going to England will become commonplace in our family," Lalaji said, to no one in particular. "After Amolak Ram, Daulat Ram, and after Daulat Ram, Balwant Rai, then Raj Kanwar, Romesh Chander, and Gopal Krishan. Each of my sons will be England-returned, each of them will have a bungalow and a motorcar. But I won't be there to live in the bungalows or ride in the motorcars."

As Daddyji was getting into his compartment, Lalaji unexpectedly caught him by the arm and said, "Amolak Ram, keep your head over your two shoulders." Before Daddyji could respond, Lalaji was gone.

Daddyji stowed his blanket and trunk on the luggage rack and leaned out the window. Everyone was calling out "*Namaste!*" and over the jumble of voices and the throb of the engine he heard Bhabiji's voice, weak but distinct, calling, "Don't come back with a memsahib! And don't forget your promise not to drink and smoke!"

Upon arriving in Bombay, Daddyji went to the offices of the various shipping agents. They all said he would have to wait months for a berth—all except Mackinnon, Mackenzie & Co., who advertised weekly P. & O. mail boats to London. They informed him that their ships were booked up for a year, but said that because very occasionally, at the eleventh hour, a passenger fell ill or died, they would take his name, provided he paid the fare in advance and was prepared to leave on twenty-four hours' notice. He paid the fare and visited Mackinnon, Mackenzie & Co. every day. Magically, after a week, a berth fell vacant on the S.S. Merkara, which was bound for Plymouth via Marseille.

He was assigned a lower berth in a small cabin for four. As he entered the cabin, he took one look and almost stepped back in surprise. On one of the lower berths was a tall, handsome Sikh, his bare feet up and his unwashed hair sticking out of the top of his loosely tied turban. He was sucking a mango, and he sat on a huge half-opened bedroll, complete with pallet, quilt, sheets, and pillows, which had been spread out on his neatly made-up berth, and which overflowed onto the floor of the cabin. The rest of the floor space was taken up by provisions—a greasy tin of ghi, a bulky canister of sweetmeats, a big, battered wooden box with compartments full of spices and condiments, and a partly torn burlap sack of aging onions.

Daddyji introduced himself, and somehow picked his way to the other lower berth and sat down. His eyes began to smart from the fumes of the onions. "Sardarji," he said to the Sikh, "make an offering of these onions to the sea, with a prayer for a safe, calm voyage."

"Doctor Sahib, these first-class onions have already journeyed with me for a thousand miles from Amritsar, and they are coming with me to Canada," the Sikh said.

Two elegant Pathans, dressed in silks, silently entered the cabin, climbed into the upper berths, and started conversing in Pushtu.

The first morning at sea, Daddyji opened his eyes and saw the Sikh standing in front of the cabin washbasin and brushing his teeth with a familiar orange toothbrush.

"Oy, Sardarji, that's my toothbrush you're using!" Daddyji called out to him.

"How could that be, Doctor Sahib?" the Sikh said, with the toothbrush in his mouth. "Don't you see that the ship has given each of its passengers soap and a towel? This is the ship's toothbrush and toothpaste."

Later that morning, Daddyji bought himself a new toothbrush at the ship's canteen.

There were forty Indian passengers on the ship, all of them new to the sea. It was now the monsoon, and high winds churned the sea into huge waves, which lashed the ship and washed across the upper decks. All the Indians were seasick, and most of them blamed their condition on the ship's English cooking. Daddyji tried to disabuse them of the idea, only to find that, because he was a doctor and was fluent in English, they had designated him leader of a delegation to carry their culinary grievances to the captain.

The captain received the delegation one midmorning, and asked them if they would care to join him in a round of beer. A couple of the delegates were Muslim and were insulted by the captain's invitation; the rest of them were sworn teetotallers and were horrified.

Daddyji, who had been brought up hearing Manji recite, "A drunkard falls over his threshold, vomits up his insides, beats his wife and children, and dies a pauper, despised and dishonored," and who had been a stalwart in college temperance societies, explained as politely as he could the revulsion that the captain's kind offer aroused in the delegation.

The captain, who was a fat Englishman with a muscular neck and a jovial expression, chuckled, got himself a beer, sat back, and heard them out.

They told him that they wanted Indian food.

"In principle, I have no objection to Indian food," he replied. "But my cooks don't know anything about it. Even if they did, some of the European passengers might find the smell offensive."

It was eventually decided that the Indians would find cooks among the Indian sailors to prepare Indian food, and that, to permit the dining room to be aired, the Indians would eat and be out half an hour before the European passengers sat down to their meals.

From then on, curries, pilaf, and parathas started coming forth from the ship's kitchen. But still, day after day, most of the Indians, including Daddyji and the two Pathans, lay sick in their berths, unable even to walk to the dining room. Not so the Sikh, who, informing Daddyji that the ship owed him his meals and that he wasn't going to allow the captain to short-change him with all this rolling and pitching, would march off to the dining room for his hard-won Indian meal.

When the ship finally made port at Aden, some of the Indian passengers, ignoring the assurances of experienced European travellers that from that point on it would be smooth sailing, cancelled their passage to England and started arranging for the long voyage back to India. Daddyji used his time in Aden to write a detailed letter to Lalaji, in which he dwelt on the vastness of the ocean, the grandeur of the ship, the diversity of the passengers, the rustic provinciality of the Sikh, and the affability of the captain, who, though a drunkard, was a true gentleman.

They left Aden the next day, and, once the ship had passed through the Suez Canal, it glided along like a toy boat on a pond. Daddyji played deck tennis, strolled on the promenade deck, sat in a deck chair, and watched the magnificent Mediterranean sunsets. Just before the ship put in at Marseille, the purser posted a bulletin on the ship's notice board announcing that a fierce storm was brewing in the Bay of Biscay, and that passengers could disembark at Marseille and proceed to London by rail and Channel boat at the cost of four guineas. Most of the remaining Indian passengers got off at Marseille, but not Daddyji. He had decided to husband his funds.

He spent an afternoon walking about Marseille, and was shocked to discover that Frenchmen, instead of keeping their shoulders steady and talking only with their mouths, as he had been taught to do, gesticulated with their bodies, waving their hands and arms about wildly, like monkeys. With relief, he got back on the ship, and he took the Bay of Biscay like a good sailor, having become used to rough seas in the Indian Ocean.

Twenty-one days after leaving Bombay, Daddyji stepped ashore at Plymouth. He was soon on a train to London, looking out eagerly at country cottages with well-kept gardens and children waving handkerchiefs from windows, and thinking how different it all was from a train journey in India, where children relieved themselves along the tracks.

He reached Victoria Station in the evening. He got down with his Dhariwal blanket and his steel trunk, and only when he was actually on the platform, shivering in the damp, did he realize that he didn't know where to go. He didn't know a soul in England, he didn't have a single introduction, he had no place to stay, and he had not been admitted to a university.

Suddenly, someone had taken his hand and was shaking it.

"You must be Ram Chand Chopra," the stranger said, smiling. He was an Indian.

"How I wish I were," Daddyji said. "I am only Amolak Ram Mehta."

The stranger laughed, and introduced himself as Mr. Chatterji, the secretary of the Indian Students' Hostel of the Y.M.C.A. in London.

"Then you must know Mr. Ralia Ram, the secretary of the Y.M.C.A. in Lahore," Daddyji said. "I used to play Ping-Pong with him."

While they were talking, a small, dark, bespectacled Indian came up. He, Daddyji quickly learned, was Ram Chand Chopra. He was on his way to Scotland and was going to stay at the Indian Students' Hostel.

"Hail fellows well met!" Daddyji said. "I carry my luck with me wherever I go!" He immediately made arrangements with Mr. Chatterji to stay at the Indian Students' Hostel himself, and Mr. Chatterji ushered his two compatriots into a cab.

Daddyji's first glimpse of London was at twilight, and he marvelled at the city's magical openness—its parks and squares, its splendid streets, unencumbered with the poor and the deformed, and its sharp, intoxicating air. He quoted to his companions, as they rode along Hyde Park, a couplet of the Punjabi poet Falak: *"Tu bhi badal, Falak,/ Ke zamana badal giya"* ("You also change, Falak, because the times have changed").

THE INDIAN STUDENTS' HOSTEL—or Shakespeare Hut, as it was called, because the site had originally been intended to accommodate a Shakespeare Memorial Theatre, marking the three-hundredth anniversary of the poet's death—was a temporary structure that had been put up during the First World War for soldiers on leave from the front. Mr. Chatterji showed Daddyji through the communal rooms—a big central lounge with a high ceiling and a huge fireplace, in which a log fire blazed, filling the room with good cheer; a dining room; and a lecture hall—and then led him to a honeycomb of cells for individual students, in the rear. He installed Daddyji in a cubicle with a table, a chair, a bed, and a small bookrack. Along the asbestos-board walls and below the ceiling were uninsulated pipes, hot to the touch, and Daddyji warmed himself at them. Then he took a hot shower in a clean, modern bathroom just outside his door, and went down the hall to take a second look at a notice board he had passed earlier. Pinned to it was a list of the hostel's forthcoming Sunday lecturers: "Lord Reading, the Viceroy-Designate of India. . . . Rabindranath Tagore, the poet. . . . Sarojini Naidu, 'the Nightingale of India.'"

Subsequent days in London were filled with discoveries: the fishmongers, the flower sellers, the dustmen, all speaking English and walking and talking with a dignity unknown to laborers in India; newspaper sellers trusting their customers to pick up their newspapers and leave their money in a hat; the shopwindows, with life-size mannequins wearing the latest fashions (the women so real, and sometimes in such a state of undress, that he had to avert his eyes) ; the polite shop assistants selling merchandise for fixed prices; the red double-decker buses, and the race for the front seat on the top deck; trains, clean and beautiful, and running underground with unimaginable frequency; the Houses of Parliament and Big Ben, Kew Gardens, and Hampton Court, all pages of history come to life; the British Museum, the Natural History Museum, Madame Tussaud's—oh, Madame Tussaud's!—and Hyde Park, and the Serpentine, right in the middle of the city; the Speakers' Corner, near Marble Arch, where people regularly denounced the government, and even the royal family; the long August twilights; the rain, such wonderful rain, not the torrents of the monsoon but a gentle, caressing drizzle; his first English purchase, a waterproof that also served as an overcoat. These things—how could he ever get used to them? How could he ever forget them?

Shakespeare Hut was conveniently situated at the corner of Keppel Street and Gower Street, within easy reach of the tube stations of Tottenham Court Road, Euston Square, and Warren Street. It was just behind the British Museum, near University College.

Daddyji intended to take a Diploma in Public Health, and he went to seek admission to University College, in its Department of Public Health, where he was interviewed by the registrar. The registrar was brittle and discouraging, but Daddyji showed him Colonel Sutherland's testimonial anyway.

"The competition is exceptionally keen for admission to University College just now," the registrar said. "The war veterans from the Medical Corps are clamoring for the few places we have in the Department of Public Health. You might stand a better chance at some other college, less well-known than ours. However, if you wish, you may go and see our Professor Henry Kenwood. He has the authority to admit candidates for the Diploma in Public Health."

Professor Kenwood turned out to be a kindly gentleman with a soft spot for the boys from the Empire. Daddyji once again brought out Colonel Sutherland's testimonial, and this time also displayed a couple of college medals he had won, in surgery and in forensic medicine and toxicology. "I had my heart set on surgery, sir, and had hoped one day to be able to write Fellow of the Royal College of Surgeons after my name," he said. "But for an F.R.C.S. I would need three years in England, and also private capital to establish a practice in India, and, you see, I am the eldest son of the eldest son in the family, so I must help educate all my brothers and cousins and nephews. I must qualify myself and get a well-paying government job quickly. My hygiene professor at King Edward Medical College, Colonel William Forster, is a man of great foresight, and he told me that if I come back from London with a public-health diploma, there will be a job waiting for me in the new Public Health Department of the Punjab."

Professor Kenwood listened to Daddyji with a barely perceptible smile. Then he said, "Young man, you'll go far. I'll see to it that you're admitted."

Daddyji could afford to stay only a year in England, and so, without the knowledge of the university authorities, he began working simultaneously in two institutions—University College, for the Diploma in Public Health, and the London School of Tropical Medicine, for the Diploma in Tropical Medicine and Hygiene. The two schools were housed in separate buildings, which, as it happened, were both quite close to Shakespeare Hut, and he devised a system of going in the morning, after a light breakfast, to University College, getting himself marked present, and then dashing over to the School of Tropical Medicine, where he would spend the rest of the day working in the laboratories. At noon, he would go to a nearby restaurant and get fish and chips and a glass of milk at the cost of a shilling and sixpence. He would have a frugal dinner in the dining room of Shakespeare Hut and spend the evenings studying. Occasionally, he would have a snack of Ovaltine at bedtime, and some fruit he had picked up at Shearn's, a fruit shop in Tottenham Court Road.

Daddyji became a protégé of one of his lecturers at the School of Tropical Medicine—Dr. Louis Westenra Sambon, an Italian, who was associated with the discovery that malaria is carried by anopheles mosquitoes. He was a short, well-built man with a fierce mustache, and he spoke in a soft voice with an Italian accent. One evening, he invited Daddyji to his house for dinner, and Daddyji took the tube from Tottenham Court Road, arriving twenty minutes later at Dr. Sambon's house, in Fordwych Road, in a quiet neighborhood. Dr. Sambon introduced Daddyji to his wife, a short, delicate Engishwoman with a doll-like face, and to his three young daughters, Stella, Dini, and Nita, all of whom were good-looking and smartly dressed, and who chattered away in a mixture of English, French, and Italian.

When everyone was seated at the dinner table, the Doctor, with great ceremony, went down to his cellar and brought back a bottle of wine. "A dinner without wine is like a day without sunshine," he said sonorously, and he opened the bottle with much ado while Daddyji stared in a mixture of fascination and apprehension. Dr. Sambon gave a short speech on the differences in the vineyards of Italy, France, and Germany; extolled the merits of various wines and vintages; and, observing that this particular wine was the most venerable of Tuscany and that it had been brought out in honor of his young guest, poured him the first glass.

Daddyji declined, first politely and then, as the Doctor pressed him, desperately.

"I confess that I am surprised that someone who is twenty-four years old and a doctor should be afraid of a little wine," Dr. Sambon said. He got up from the table, went upstairs, and returned with a sleepy child of about six. "Here, Arthur, have a glass of wine," he said, and, as Daddyji looked on in horror, the child happily downed the glass.

WHEN DADDYJI had been at Shakespeare Hut for a few months, he heard about a lodging house nearby, in Tavistock Square, where for only a little more money he could get a larger and much quieter room than his cubicle. He went around to the house, which had a sign in the window reading, "Bed and Breakfast. Colonials Welcome." The door was opened by a stout lady in an apron. "*Ach, so,*" she said, catching her breath. "New boarder, *ja?* How *do* you do?" She led him upstairs. "My maid knocks at your door at eight o'clock and leaves your breakfast." She showed him a vacant room, which had a gas heater and afforded a view of the grassy lawn and the beds of daffodils in the middle of the square. She led him down the hall to the bathroom and indicated a water closet and a bathtub with a geyser, impressing upon him that he must not linger in his bath. "It's the only one in the house." She added with pride, "All my gentlemen can afford coppers for the geyser."

"I'm a fully qualified doctor," Daddyji said. "I'm very particular about my reputation, and that of the house in which I live."

She assured him that her establishment had a good

name, for she took only nice, well-spoken colonials. "*Ach, Herr Doktor*, my lodgers are everything to me. Ever since my husband goes to America and never sends for me since ten years, my life is my lodgers. And how hard do I work to get him out of Bohemia!"

As soon as Daddyji moved into the room, the landlady gave him a key to the park gate, and a folding chair, which on an occasional fine weekend he would carry down and set up in the park, so that he could read in the sun. He faithfully kept to his regimen of fish and chips, dinner at Shakespeare Hut, and fruit from Shearn's—though now, being better at budgeting, he sometimes supplemented his fruit at bedtime with bread and butter, eggs, or almonds. In addition to his work in classrooms, laboratories, and libraries, he spent long hours in outdoor clinics and on field trips to reservoirs, slaughterhouses, and other places of interest to students of public health. He forwent not only the common diversions like cinemas, dance halls, and girls (he was afraid of entanglements with English girls) but also sports and games.

The landlady had three other "gentlemen" in her establishment, and they were all Punjabis and all from rich homes. One was a Muslim who was studying at the Inns of Court and called himself a nawab, and the others were Sikhs who were training to be railway engineers and called themselves maharajas. The three made the most of their time in London, going out every night and returning home drunk. Although when they were sober they treated Daddyji almost like an elder— after all, he was a doctor and a postgraduate student— when they were inebriated they would taunt him for being "a swot, a puritan, and a provincial." Their greatest excesses were reserved for Saturday night, which they called "a golden night of libation." After one of these nights, the three bounded into Daddyji's room, where he sat propped up against his pillows reading a textbook, and gathered around him and started singing, in rousing, discordant voices, "For he's a jolly good fellow." They tried to force him to drink from a bottle of whiskey, splashing some on his nose and chin. Daddyji squirmed out of the way. The nawab snatched the bottle from the others, took a few steps backward, and hurled it at Daddyji. The bottle whistled past his ear, sailed out the window, and shattered on the pavement below.

"Do you realize you could have killed me?" Daddyji shouted at the three rowdies, who were now squabbling among themselves.

The landlady came thumping into the room. She was in nightgown, cap, and slippers, and was followed by a tall, helmeted constable.

"What you are thinking you're up to?" she cried out. "That bottle! Who throws it? Which one? Disgrace! A policeman, in *my* establishment!"

The nawab and the maharajas stared dumbly at Daddyji, who, however, said nothing.

"Madam, perhaps this is a matter for the police," the constable said. "Allow me to take charge."

He turned to Daddyji. "Whose room is this?"

Daddyji, with a flourish, produced his visiting card, which read, "Amolak Ram Mehta, Bachelor of Medicine, Bachelor of Surgery; Member of British Medical Association."

The constable saluted him respectfully. "All the same, sir, if I may—I think someone should go down promptly and sweep up the broken glass. If a passerby should chance to step on it, we might have a nasty accident on our hands."

One of the maharajas seized Daddyji's hairbrush and ran downstairs to tidy up the pavement, while the nawab offered the constable a chair and told him, "My father, Khan Sahib, is deputy inspector general of police in Peshawar. You may be knowing his assistant. He's an Englishman, Irwin Smith."

"Know Irwin! Irwin is my brother!" the constable cried.

The nawab gave the constable a cigarette and a drink, and the constable assured his new friends and the landlady that none of them would be charged with disorderly conduct. But before he left he pocketed a pound from each of the lodgers, suavely observing, "You mustn't be allowed to get off scot-free."

DADDYJI WALKED into the lounge of Shakespeare Hut one day and was startled to see a friend from Lahore—Mohammed Saleem, the perennial tennis champion of India—sitting in a corner playing bridge. Being fair of complexion, he looked very much at home in Savile Row tweeds, as dashing, handsome, and trim as ever. "Sahibji!" Daddyji cried.

Saleem jumped up and shook his hand. "Just in London for a few weeks," Saleem said. "Glad to see you." He went back to his game.

It was just like Saleem not to inquire why Daddyji was in London; he took it for granted that people he met in India would pop up in England, and the other way around. He maintained a house in Lahore and a flat off Piccadilly, and, being a bachelor and a senior advocate of the Punjab High Court (he was about ten years older than Daddyji), he was able to come and go as he pleased. Daddyji had first met Saleem at the summer house of Rai Bahadur Gokal Chand Malhotra, a Punjabi notable. The house was in a town on the road to Simla, and Daddyji, who was on vacation from medical college at the time, was tutoring the Rai Bahadur's two grandsons in English while Saleem, who was also on vacation, was tutoring them in tennis. Daddyji had always regarded tennis as a game for sissies—much inferior to the heartier and more rugged sport of hockey—but with Saleem on the court the game had drama, excitement, grace, toughness, and an aesthetic quality Daddyji had never imagined possible. Saleem gave Daddyji an old Slazenger racquet and taught him how to play, and by the end of the vacation Daddyji had become a lifelong devotee of the game. Ever since, Saleem—who had not only the grand, romantic manner of a real nawab but also the impeccable English speech of a Cambridge man—had been Daddyji's North Star. Now, in London, Daddyji saw Saleem often at the hostel, playing bridge. He was as dazzling at the card table as he was on the tennis court. He would bid cautiously but play with bold assurance. If the bid went to his opponent, he would be dogged in his defense, but if he had won the bid he would scrutinize the dummy and, after two or three tricks, throw in his hand and say, "The rest are mine." They invariably were. Between rubbers, or when Saleem was dummy, he would give Daddyji an occasional lesson, and Daddyji came to think of cards as being, like tennis, a diversion of the successful and civilized man—though for the time being he contented himself with Ping-Pong.

DADDYJI WAS at Shakespeare Hut to hear a Sunday lecture. A Dr. Bhattacharji, who was in the audience, and whom Daddyji knew slightly, took him aside. "I don't mind telling you that Mrs. Bhattacharji and I have never known a young man as attractive and as winning as you," Dr. Bhattacharji said. Daddyji had met him and his wife at other Shakespeare Hut lectures and had been quite curious about them. The Doctor was a Bengali Hindu, his wife an Anglo-Indian. She had blue eyes and a sturdy English walk but always wore saris. "I hope you'll enjoy living here as much as I have. I have a very good practice in Notting Hill Gate, but I am nearing sixty now, and I am a little asthmatic. I want to retire to some place like the South of France. What would you think of coming in as my assistant for a year or so? If you prove yourself, you could inherit an established London practice."

An established practice was something that many doctors did not achieve even after a lifetime's work, and Daddyji now imagined himself in Dr. Bhattacharji's shoes. He knew that in a working-class area like Notting Hill Gate "black doctors" were extremely popular, because in addition to knowing modern medicine they were thought to know black magic. If he stayed on in England, he would have a very lucrative career. He might have an English wife, and perhaps could even realize his ambition to become an F.R.C.S. But then he thought of his responsibilities to the family. He became aware that Dr. Bhattacharji was waiting to be thanked.

"I am honored," he said. "But I must go home and share what I've learned here. My mother used to say, 'To one who shares food it is sugar; to one who eats alone it is a toad.' "

As DADDYJI's boat train pulled out of Victoria Station, he stood at the window and looked out at the dusk falling over the sooty chimneys. He had spent eleven months in England, and things couldn't have gone better. He had in his steel trunk a Diploma in Public Health and a Diploma in Tropical Medicine and Hygiene, and now it was the turn of Daulat Ram, who had just graduated from King Edward Medical College. Daddyji had been able to arrange for Daulat Ram's admission to University College and for lodgings for him in Shakespeare Hut, and in order to save a little money for Daulat Ram's English education Daddyji had forgone a tour of Europe. Only one detail remained—to write a thank-you letter to his landlady in Tavistock Square. How he loved England, he would write. He had come to think of it as the most beautiful, the most hospitable country in the world. The colder, the grayer, the foggier the sky, the more he had liked it. He would never forget the English day breaking over good old Tavistock Square. He knew that in his long life he would visit many countries and see much, but that nothing would take the place of the haunts of his student days—Tavistock Square, Shakespeare Hut, Shearn's, the Tottenham Court Road tube station.

He arrived in Bombay on a sultry August morning and was met by Daulat Ram, who was booked to sail for England that very evening. Daddyji handed over his medical textbooks, his lecture notes, his laboratory records, his wristwatch, his pen, and thirty pounds—practically everything he had on him—to his brother.

V

ENGLAND-RETURNED

D ADDYJI'S FIRST JOB WAS IN RAWALPINDI, WHERE HE assumed the duties of municipal health officer — a couple of months after his return from London. Rawalpindi, a lovely city of about a hundred thousand, was situated in the foothills of the Punjab Himalayas and, because it was the starting point of the only route to the Vale of Kashmir, was known as the Gateway to Kashmir. All around the city were orchards of loquats, peaches, pears, and limes. Daddyji found a commodious two-story house built around a courtyard off Murree Road, in a tranquil neighborhood. He made the rooms on the ground floor into a drawing room, a dining room, and a study, and the rooms upstairs into bedrooms. He bought himself a splendid polo pony, an English saddle, several pairs of riding breeches, a riding coat, and a white sola topi.

Every morning at daybreak, Daddyji would get into his riding clothes, set his topi at a jaunty angle, mount his horse, and make his rounds of inspection, followed by a phalanx of sanitary inspectors on foot. As he trotted along, the vegetable and fruit venders who were on their way to market would salaam and draw aside for his train. He felt he was the luckiest man alive, and marvelled at the coincidences that had secured him a job with a salary of six hundred rupees a month— many times as much as Lalaji had ever earned, and considerably more than the salary of any starting officer in the élite Indian Civil Service. After reaching India, he had sought out Colonel Forster, who told him that the Punjab Public Health Department would not be set up for two more years. "There is, however, a vacancy for a municipal health officer at Pindi," Colonel Forster had said. "But I don't think you stand much of a chance. Most of the candidates are men with a great deal of experience. Still, I suppose there's no harm in your trying for it." Daddyji had rushed to Rawalpindi, seen everybody who was anybody in the municipality, and impressed upon them that he was young, energetic, and in touch with the latest discoveries in public health. He had secured the job. Now, on his morning rounds, he would look into any charges of food or drug adulteration or other violations of public-health regulations, inspect the contagious-disease hospital and the meat dealers' premises and the sweetshops, and oversee the cleaning of drains, the transport of refuse to the city dumps, and the observance of sanitary provisions at building sites. Dismounting from his horse, he would walk through lanes and *gullis*—trailed by reluctant sanitary inspectors, who considered these slums too filthy even for them, let alone their officer—and direct that a putrefying goat carcass be disinfected and removed, or that a reeking sewage bin be equipped with a cover.

In the afternoon, he would go to his office and send off a series of proposals to the city authorities: the haphazard and insanitary butchering of animals in front of tenements and vending stalls should be banned, and the municipality should build slaughterhouses on the outskirts of the city; the system of carrying refuse in open handcarts and bullock carts should be abolished, and the municipality should purchase closed lorries for the purpose; the aging, dried-up cows that had been abandoned by their owners to the city's streets should be herded together, and the municipality should build shelters for them; sweepers forced to camp in the streets should be provided with living quarters; and so on. But such proposals, however urgent and elementary, required expenditure, so they were often shelved. A city, Daddyji discovered, was unregenerate in a way that a village was not.

All Daddyji's energies were soon absorbed by the riddle of the bubonic plague. The Punjab was besieged by epidemics—cholera in the summer, bubonic plague in the winter and spring, smallpox in the spring, summer, and winter—but, of all the cities in the Punjab, Rawalpindi was the most pestilential, plague being endemic there. No one had been able to explain satisfactorily why plague did not have any significant seasonal abatement in Rawalpindi, as it had in other cities. Daddyji assumed that the explanation must lie in the godowns, or warehouses, since they were breeding grounds for rats, and rats carried fleas, which, in turn, carried *Pasteurella pestis*, the plague bacteria. He tested the atmosphere in the Rawalpindi godowns and discovered that it was exceptionally moist. He concluded that the additional moisture was enough to sustain the fleas all year round, whereas in other cities they died in the dry heat of summer. He traced the cause of the high humidity to the apples, pears, plums, cherries, and other fruits from Kashmir that were stored in the Rawalpindi godowns on their way to the markets in the plains. He set about improving storage facilities, at the same time intensifying a plague-inoculation program already in existence, and eventually plague in Rawal-pindi was arrested. His isolation of the cause of Rawal-pindi's endemic plague amounted to a scientific discovery, and it was so reported in the *British Medical Journal*.

❧

Now AND again, Mr. Henry Phillips Tollinton, the commissioner of Rawalpindi Division, would invite Daddyji to his house in the Civil Lines, where high government officials lived. The house was a large government bungalow with impressive grounds, on which Mr. Tollinton had built a couple of tennis courts. He had two daughters, close together in age and fast growing into women. They were plump and short, with plain, round faces and bulging calf muscles. Like Mr. Tollinton and Daddyji, they were keen tennis players, and the four would often pair off for doubles.

Once, His Excellency the Lieutenant Governor of the Punjab came to Rawalpindi on a tour, and Mr. Tollinton arranged a game of doubles in which Daddyji partnered His Excellency, and Mr. Tollinton partnered the deputy commissioner. At the end of two sets, the score was one all, and though Daddyji and His Excellency contested the third, and final, set hotly, they lost. Afterward, as they were all walking across the lawn to the veranda, where cane chairs and tables had been set up for refreshments, His Excellency remarked, "No matter. Mehta and I will take our revenge tomorrow at the Pindi Club."

Before Mr. Tollinton or his partner could reply, Daddyji spoke up. "Your Excellency, that is out of the question."

His Excellency caught his breath. An invitation from a superior was a command. "What's this? Why not?"

Mr. Tollinton and the deputy commissioner cast about desperately to find something to distract His Excellency's attention. Clubs had originally been established in India by the Europeans, who were few in number, and who wished to relax among their own kind. They had taken it for granted that the Indians were unclubbable. After all, their women were often in purdah, and they had all kinds of taboos about food and drink. But the Indians, especially well-placed government officers, had come to regard the European clubs as a sort of Xanadu, although they continued to be refused admission to most of them.

"Your Excellency!" cried the deputy commissioner. "Look at that remarkable pigeon up there!"

Daddyji realized that he had blundered in raising a sensitive issue in the presence of three Englishmen. "Indian civilians are not allowed on the premises of the Pindi Club," he said falteringly.

"It's all right, Your Excellency," Mr. Tollinton put in quickly. "Dr. Mehta will be most welcome at the Pindi Club."

The following day, Daddyji was made a temporary member of the club, and the four played there, but Daddyji and His Excellency again lost the match, two to one. In due course, Daddyji was elected the first permanent Indian civilian member of the Pindi Club.

❧

DADDYJI, ON HIS FIRST CHRISTMAS after returning
from England, went to Lahore to celebrate his twenty-
sixth birthday with the family. Lalaji had been transferred to Lahore in 1915. For some time, he had felt
ashamed of the way he had to earn his livelihood, because over the years the office of *patwari* had become a
symbol of corruption, and such prestige as had originally been associated with it had been eroded by the
patwaris' venality. Lalaji had often thought of giving
up his job, yet he had no more been able to find an
alternative means of support than he had been able to
go back to his ancestral occupation of village landowner. "Two poor villagers were standing on a riverbank," he would say wryly about the predicament he
was in. "One of them thought he saw a blanket floating
by, and dived for it. Soon both he and the blanket were
being carried off by the current. The man on the bank
called to the drowning man, 'Fool, come back! Let go
of the blanket—swim for your life!' The drowning man
cried, 'I want to let go of the blanket, but the blanket
won't let go of me!' You see, the man was in the grip
of a huge bear." In any event, as Lalaji had grown
older, he had felt less and less like going around in the
hot sun measuring fields. Moreover, village life had
long since lost whatever savor it might have had for
him. He had therefore gladly made the move to Lahore, where the family lived in a newly developed area
a couple of miles outside the ancient walls of the native
city; theirs was a rented house—a small brick structure
at the foot of a *gulli*, which had a little space in front
where the family's buffalo and horse were tied. In 1917,
however, Lalaji had reached the mandatory retirement

Lalaji, Lahore, 1919

age and had been pensioned off. He had tried to busy himself around the house with domestic matters, but they hadn't required much time. So he had dreamed over his hookah and taken long naps. His childhood interest in music had revived, and he had started playing the sitar in earnest, and inviting wandering minstrels into the house for impromptu musicales that sometimes turned into little feasts. The expenses in Lahore had proved to be much greater than those in the village, and without the *patwari's* emoluments the family savings had been severely strained. Lalaji had decided he would set himself up as an exporter and importer of textiles, and had asked Daddyji, when he was in London, to send samples of the latest fabrics from Manchester. Lalaji had even gone to the length of having some business stationery printed: "B. R. Mehta & Sons, Importers, Sole Agents, Commission Agents, and Manufacturers' Representatives of Cotton and Woollen Piece Goods, Fancies, Hosiery, Sundries, &c. &c., Lahore (India). London Representative: Mr. A. R. Mehta, Shakespeare Hut, Keppel Street, London, W.C. 1." But the stationery had merely gathered dust in a corner, and so had a parcel of swatches sent by Daddyji.

Now, in Lahore, Daddyji entered the little house; went straight to Lalaji, who sat enthroned at the head of a charpoy, pulling at his hookah; took from his pocket a thousand rupees in new banknotes, which he had saved from his salary; and tried to press them into Lalaji's hand.

Lalaji, with a casual glance, waved them aside.

Bhabiji stepped forward joyfully with tears in her eyes and held out her veil. Lalaji looked the other way, and Daddyji placed the banknotes in it. She shyly folded her veil around the notes, and as the younger children, who had been waiting to pay their respects to Daddyji, surrounded him with a clamor, she slipped the little bundle under the bedclothes at the foot of the charpoy.

Daddyji changed out of his Western suit into his comfortable pajamas and collarless shirt, and while he was sitting on the floor in the kitchen with the family eating the midday meal, the wife of a neighbor walked in and said to Bhabiji, "Where is the England-returned? I would like to see an England-returned before I die."

Bhabiji waved a hand toward Daddyji.

"England-returned!" the neighbor exclaimed. "And sitting on the floor, eating with his fingers! Why go all the way to England for that?"

Just before Daddyji returned to Rawalpindi, Bhabiji insisted that he take four hundred rupees out of the thousand he had given her, and buy himself a tonga and harness worthy of his pony. When he got back to Rawalpindi, he did as she had asked. He retained Tika Ram, a tall, thin syce, who belonged to a community of grooms from the eastern part of the United Provinces; the forebears of these grooms, it was said, had taken part in the Mutiny, but subsequently, as if to atone for this deed, they and their descendants had dedicated themselves to looking after Englishmen's horses, especially their polo ponies. Tika Ram kept the rig polished and the pony well groomed. Although Daddyji still rode the pony on his morning rounds, in the late afternoons Tika Ram hitched it to the tonga, and Daddyji drove around in the tonga with Tika Ram at his

Bhabiji, Lahore, 1919

side ready to catch the reins and wait whenever Daddyji jumped down for a call. Out in the open, Daddyji let the pony gallop along the rutted roads. The bumpier the tonga ride, the more excited he felt; he was optimistic, young, handsome, and a bachelor, and he was courted by the small official community of British and Indians.

Soon after Daddyji's visit to Lahore, Bhabiji came to stay with him, bringing with her Haru Ram's son Jaswant and Daddyji's brothers Balwant, Raj Kanwar, Romesh, and Krishan, who ranged in age from nineteen to seven. Lalaji remained behind, because he didn't want to go where he would be known merely as his son's father. When Daddyji was at work in the office, Tika Ram would drive the children around in the tonga, or convey them to Topi Park, and when Daddyji came home, he would get Bhabiji to dress up in her best clothes and together they would take the air in the tonga, often taking Krishan with them; he was an intelligent and inquisitive child with artistic leanings, and was a special favorite of Daddyji's. As they rode through the Civil Lines, Daddyji would tell Bhabiji about England, and she would listen to him, sitting very straight and never taking her eyes off his face. Bhaji Ganga Ram and Chhoti Bhabiji were also there, and for a couple of months all of them lived in the house like a family in a village.

When Daddyji was at King Edward Medical College, Bhaji Ganga Ram had begun studying to be a lawyer, for he had become dissatisfied with being superintendent of Quadrangle; the job had a fixed salary of a hundred rupees a month and no prospects for advancement. He had passed the first part of the two-part law examination but failed the second, and, as a partly qualified lawyer, had been able to apply for the position of sub-judge to a panel of High Court judges in Lahore, who made their selection on the basis of the applicants' deportment and dress. Daddyji, who had worn Western clothes for years, had given him a few lessons in how to comport himself like a sahib, and when Bhaji Ganga Ram was going for his interview with the High Court judges, Daddyji had tied his best tie around his uncle's neck and had also given him his best belt to hold up a brand-new pair of Western trousers. Bhaji Ganga Ram, whatever sartorial discomfort he may have felt, had impressed the judges and had got the job. As it happened, he was posted to Rawalpindi. When Daddyji first arrived there, he discovered that Bhaji Ganga Ram and Chhoti Bhabiji were living in a small house in a narrow *gulli*, and he prevailed on them to move in with him and share his bungalow.

They lived together amicably for a time. Then, one evening, Daddyji went to dine at the house of a friend who was an advocate. The advocate told Daddyji that Bhaji Ganga Ram had alienated most of the members of the Rawalpindi Bar Association. "He's upright and fair-minded, but in court he's overbearing and sarcastic," the advocate said. "He's constantly reprimanding the advocates who plead before him at the bench, just as if they were his boarders at Quadrangle—as, indeed, many of them were. He has become one of the most unpopular men in Rawalpindi, and if he doesn't mend his ways, we'll petition the High Court for his transfer."

When Daddyji dutifully reported the conversation

Daddyji, Lahore, 1921

to Bhaji Ganga Ram, Bhaji Ganga Ram said, in his usual stiff manner, "People's opinions change like the wind, but principles are founded on bedrock. I have always put my principles above my ambition, and I would advise you to do the same."

A few days later, just after Bhabiji and the children had gone back to Lahore, Daddyji was in his room packing his shoes and tennis whites in a canvas bag for a game at the Pindi Club when he heard Bhaji Ganga Ram declaiming a famous Urdu couplet in the next room: *"Bane is qadar mukazib kabhi ghar ka munh na dekha./Kati umar hotlon men mare hasptal ja kar"* ("He became so very civilized that he never saw the face of home. He spent his life in hotels and died in hospital").

At the time, Daddyji didn't pay much attention, but when he came home from the club he found, to his surprise, that Bhaji Ganga Ram and Chhoti Bhabiji didn't return his greeting. Afterward, however often Daddyji tried to speak to them, they ignored him. Bhaji Ganga Ram would turn his back and walk away, and when Daddyji met Chhoti Bhabiji in a passageway, she would avert her face. Though Daddyji repeatedly invited them to join him at the table, they would not do so. Chhoti Bhabiji set up separate cooking facilities, and they ate in their room. The rupture became family knowledge when Bhaji Ganga Ram pointedly did not ask Daddyji to the wedding of Chhoti Bhabiji's brother Vidya Rattan.

One day, Bhaji Ganga Ram silently handed Daddyji a letter he had received from Daulat Ram, who wrote from London that he had been hospitalized with a severe case of dysentery and that he was short of funds; he asked Bhaji Ganga Ram for a loan of five hundred rupees. Daddyji immediately sold his English microscope and cabled the money to Daulat Ram, scolding him for writing to Bhaji Ganga Ram in the first place. "Your education is my responsibility," he wrote, "and I don't see how you think Bhaji Ganga Ram comes into it."

Since Daddyji found little cheer at home, with Bhaji Ganga Ram and Chhoti Bhabiji living under his roof like strangers, he started spending more and more time at the Pindi Club. It was situated in the Civil Lines and had a large clubhouse, cricket and hockey grounds, and cottages in which members could stay. Every afternoon around four, when Daddyji had finished his work, he would go there, play a few sets of tennis or innings of cricket, bathe, change, and join some English friends for a drink—they would drink whiskey-and-soda while he drank lemon squash. He would often stay on for dinner, and sometimes, on his way home, he would put in a quick appearance at the City Club, which had been founded by Indians in retaliation for the Pindi Club. (Its constitution prohibited members from even entertaining Europeans as guests.) Here he would listen to stories told at the expense of Englishmen. "I once prosecuted a case in front of one of them," someone would say. "It was a case of camel lifting. The white sahib couldn't even understand what the offense was, and I explained to him that the camel did not belong to the accused but was stolen property. So you know what he said? 'Bring the camel into this court, and

show me how the accused—though I grant you he
looks like a strong fellow—can possibly lift it.'"

When Daddyji had been in Rawalpindi about a
year, Bhaji Ganga Ram was transferred, upon the petition of the Bar Association, and posted to Jagadhri, a
small station in the district of Ambala, and Daddyji's
own stay in Rawalpindi was cut short as a result of an
announcement he saw in the *Tribune*, an English-
language daily, advertising an "All-India Competition"
for half a dozen Rockefeller Foundation Fellowships
in the United States. Here was a chance of going to the
New World, he thought, and making up for lost op-
portunities; he had regretted not having spent more
time in the West. But if he applied and was selected,
he would have to give up his job and its unheard-of
salary, which was the family standby. Balwant, Jaswant, and Raj Kanwar were now all at Government
College, Romesh was just about to enter it, and Krishan
was doing exceptionally well in school. Daulat Ram
had finished his education in England and had returned home some time earlier but had not been able
to find a job. Despite all this, Daddyji could not resist
the temptation. He applied, and was awarded a fellowship. He resigned his post in Rawalpindi and went to
Lahore to say his goodbyes.

VI

TRAVELLING
FELLOW

D ADDYJI HAD JUST PASSED THE PORT OF ADEN AND was in the Red Sea. He settled down in his cabin with a letter from Lalaji, who had enjoined him not to read it until the ship had left the waters of the Indian Ocean. On the envelope Lalaji had written, in his elegant Urdu script, "Most of my life is behind me, and, provided I live, we shall meet. But, as we say in our beloved Punjab, 'Even the meeting of rivulets is a matter of kismet.'"

Daddyji tore open the envelope and started reading the letter. (He destroyed the letter in 1938, along with most of the family records, but it is preserved in his memory.) Lalaji began by remarking that his great-grandfather, grandfather, and father had all lived and died in the same little village of Nawankote. His great-grandfather had gone on foot as far as the next important village, and that was all. His grandfather had been on a pilgrimage to Hardwar by bullock cart, and that had taken several months. His father, however, had been a passenger on the first train between Lahore and Saharanpur, and that journey had taken only a couple of days. And he, Lalaji, had ridden in a motorcar, and his sons had crossed the oceans in steamships—something his own father could not have dreamed of. Yet he had no trouble at all imagining the children of his children flying about the continents in airplanes. The world, which had once moved through time like an elephant, was now racing like a gazelle. He said that after his death it would fall upon Daddyji to see that every last member of the family received an education if he deserved it. He hoped that the name of the family would be known far and wide, and that people would marvel and say, "Look where they started, and look where they've reached!" He would have Daddyji remember that they were their father's sons, but that they must also be their sons' fathers. "Amolak Ram," Daddyji read, "I ask one thing of you—to banish from the family memory that I was ever a *patwari*. This burden of your father's should not pass to your children, or to your children's children." Thereafter, Lalaji's career was never mentioned by the family, and the silence was broken only forty years later. By then, the word "*patwari*" had ceased to mean anything to a generation born and bred in modern cities. "I am writing all this now because I have a premonition that I will not see you again," Lalaji's letter concluded. "Before you return, I will be dead."

Daddyji walked over to the porthole and looked out at the sea. Lalaji had never expressed himself at such length before. What did his presentiment mean? He was then around sixty, and in good health. There was every reason to suppose that he would have a long life. As a man of science, Daddyji could not take premonitions seriously; probably Lalaji's intimations of his own death meant no more than that he was apprehensive about Daddyji's going away on a long journey. Yet he felt guilty, a victim of kismet himself, for, just before he left, news had come that Daulat Ram had missed succeeding him in his job in Rawalpindi. Daddyji had been so confident that Daulat Ram would get the job that he had presented him with the horse and tonga, and now they had had to be sold to raise money for Lalaji and the family. This ill omen, falling as it did on the eve of his departure, had cast a shadow over the voyage.

BEFORE DADDYJI could get accustomed to the white tallness of New York, to the informality of the Rockefeller Foundation representatives, or to the mechanical wonder that whisked him up twenty-six floors to the Foundation offices, he was shunted off to Baltimore, where he started working for a doctorate in public health at Johns Hopkins. Each morning, he would settle at his table in the laboratory, pull his microscope toward him, inhale the cloying odor of formaldehyde, and look around at the rows of shiny tabletops, with their test tubes, microscopes, and dissection sets. This was clearly the world he had been destined for all along. He would take his degree, become a professor at Johns Hopkins, and buy a house in Baltimore. He would send for the entire family, establish them all in his house, and enter his brothers in American schools and colleges. He would get Bhabiji an electric sewing machine and show America to her and Lalaji in a Model T Ford.

One morning, he bent over the microscope, inserted a slide of an anopheles mosquito, and started doing a dissection.

"How's it going, Mehta?" asked the laboratory instructor, coming up to Daddyji's table.

Daddyji showed the instructor the malaria parasite in the mosquito's stomach.

The instructor was astonished, and asked Daddyji how he had learned to recognize the parasite.

"I'm a qualified doctor. I was trained at the London School of Tropical Medicine, and I hold a Diploma in Public Health from University College, in London," Daddyji said.

"Then what are you doing here?" asked the instructor. "You're too advanced to be a student."

"I'm here to collect a doctorate in public health," Daddyji said, with a smile.

"What's the point in getting another degree? It's just a few more letters after your name," the instructor said.

A few days later, the university authorities, having been apprised of Daddyji's credentials, told him that he needed practical experience in the field more than academic work in a university, and, despite his protests, shunted him back to New York for a consultation with Foundation representatives about what he was to do next. As he was sitting in the waiting room of the Foundation offices, a secretary handed him a letter. He was about to pocket it, but then he noticed that it was from Daulat Ram and that it had been en route for more than a month. He opened it and started reading.

Daulat Ram said that after Daddyji left, Lalaji had seemed quite dejected. The fact that his eldest son, who had been so gainfully employed, had given up his job had weighed upon him. Within a short time, he had contracted pneumonia—he had always called pneumonia "the old man's friend"—and died. "He had some happy moments in his last months, though," Daulat Ram wrote. "He received your letter from Bombay, from the Taj Mahal Palace Hotel, and read out to us that you were paying thirty rupees a day for your room. Bhabiji said, 'Thirty rupees a day! My son must be eating rice pudding off gold plates all day long!' Lalaji looked very pleased." Before Lalaji fell ill, Daulat Ram had got a temporary job at Kulu, a valley high up in the Punjab Himalayas. He said that he had written to Lalaji and invited him for a stay, but had had no idea that he would actually come. One evening, Daulat Ram had been taking a stroll along the track above his hill cottage when he noticed, silhouetted against the sunset, a tall man astride an Arabian horse. Having never seen an Arabian horse in the hills—the hill people rode ponies so squat that they were called "frogs"—he had assumed that the man must be a maharaja from a nearby principality. But the man had ridden up to Daulat Ram and hailed him by name. It was Lalaji. He sat very straight in the saddle, with his bedroll tied behind him. Daulat Ram seized his father's foot with joy. He said to himself that only Lalaji could have commandeered such a horse in the plains and managed to ride it over the treacherous mule trails and through the high mountain passes. Lalaji had stayed with Daulat Ram for a few weeks. "I had never been free with Lalaji—who had?—and I like to think this was an occasion that brought us closer," Daulat Ram wrote. But, as usual, Lalaji had kept very much to himself, though he had seemed busy and cheerful. Every morning, he would meditate, go for his ablutions to a stream nearby, and then take a walk into the copse above the cottage to gather unfamiliar mountain herbs. When Daulat Ram went to work, Lalaji would sometimes go with

him and stop off at the bazaar, where he would ask
the local herbalist about the medicinal properties of the
herbs and the possibility of transplanting them to the
plains. He would spend the evening in the cottage,
concocting remedies, which he tested on himself. He
made a chutney out of one plant and ate it to see if it
would improve his memory. He took the flowers and
leaves of another plant in candied form as a laxative
and in tea as an expectorant. He had become concerned
about his health, but as far as Daulat Ram could tell,
he was as fit as ever. He rode back down to the plains
by himself.

Daddyji went to his hotel in a daze, flung himself
across the bed, and sobbed into the pillow. It was the
first time he had cried as a man. He remembered one
of the last conversations he had had with Lalaji. Daddyji had started growing a mustache, and Lalaji had
made a sarcastic remark about its thin, straggly appearance. Daddyji had said irritably, "I'm not a child any-
more, I'm a man." Turning away, Lalaji had retorted,
"So you think you're a man now."

FROM NEW YORK, the Foundation dispatched Daddyji to some marshes near Richmond, Virginia, to learn
the latest techniques of malaria control. When he was
changing trains at Union Station in Washington, he
noticed that the cars of his new train were marked
"Whites Only" and "Blacks Only." He was confused,
and, not wanting to create a scene by boarding the
wrong car, he rushed up to a conductor and asked him
where he should go.

The conductor stared at him. "Straight hair, straight nose, brown skin—a half-breed?"

"Indian from India, sir."

"Hindu? You're white."

At the station in Richmond, Daddyji was met by a local physician who was a malaria specialist. "I'm mighty glad to see you," the physician said. "I feared that you might be black. Glad you aren't, or we'd have had a devil of a time getting you into a hotel. Sure is nice that you aren't black."

After working on malaria control not only in Richmond but also in Sardinia, where the Foundation was helping the Italian government to rid the island of mosquitoes, Daddyji spent a year in various hospitals in Britain, studying the etiology of tuberculosis. He had become interested in the disease a few years earlier, when one of Bibi Parmeshwari Devi's young daughters, Vidya, developed it in the bones of her hands; both hands were disfigured, she was in constant pain, and it was taken for granted that because of this physical defect she would be a spinster all her life.

Toward the end of the second year of his fellowship (the grant had been extended to cover two years), Daddyji sat down in his lodgings in London and wrote a momentous letter to Daulat Ram, who in the meantime had become a district health officer in Lahore. "I have made up my mind to settle in England," he wrote. "I am sending you a trunk with all my old clothes, which I won't be needing now, since I shall be buying new ones, more appropriate for an English doctor. Here, during consultation, a doctor must wear a short black coat and striped trousers. To be better prepared for general practice here, I am now working as a clinical assistant to a Bengali doctor who has a surgery in Paddington." He said that he had saved a large part of his fellowship allowance, which he thought would be quite enough to make an initial payment toward the purchase of a London practice, and that he was keeping his eye out for advertisements in the *British Medical Journal* of practices for sale. He had also advertised for a corner house in Hendon, where some friends of his had promised him an introduction to the community. "Once I have a home in London, all our brothers can come by turns to England for their education," he said. "In the meantime, as long as you are on the spot, I have nothing to worry about. Between you and me, if one lives in England there's no harm even in taking an English wife."

Posting the letter filled him with the same exhilaration he had felt when he ran away to Bombay twelve years before. London was more bewitching than ever, and the more time he spent there, the more at home he felt.

Soon after he had sent off the letter, a young Englishwoman came to the Paddington surgery complaining of pain in her bladder. As Daddyji was recording her medical history, she broke down. "As a matter of fact, there's nothing wrong with my bladder," she said. "I'm pregnant. I don't want it. I want you to get rid of it."

Daddyji was taken aback. "You can't mean that. The word 'abortion' is not in my vocabulary. Bearing children is the highest destiny of woman."

"My husband doesn't think so."

"Does he love you? Do you love him?"

"Yes, but he's an Indian, and I don't want a black baby."

Daddyji pointed out to her the inconsistency of loving a man and not wanting his baby, whereupon she called in her husband, who had been sitting in the waiting room, and who thereupon argued the case for abortion with all the passion of his wife.

Daddyji was appalled. He sat back in his chair and looked at the couple. The girl was pale, with blue eyes and long blond hair, and the man was a swarthy South Indian, with thick lips, a snub nose, and kinky hair. Daddyji said to himself that if this was the fate of mixed marriages and of Indians transplanted to England, perhaps he should go home after all and marry a girl of his own caste. Together they could produce pure Kshatriya babies, who would grow up in a stable Hindu society.

During a brief stay in Dublin, Daddyji went to a local cinema to see "Robin Hood," starring Douglas Fairbanks. When it was over, the young man sitting in the next seat turned to him and said, "Wasn't that a smashing picture?" He added, shaking hands, "I'm La Touche." The acquaintanceship so struck up in the theatre grew into friendship, and La Touche often invited Daddyji to his father's home—a big Georgian house with a tennis court, just outside Dublin. Once, La Touche took Daddyji to a party, and Daddyji found himself part of a circle around two tousle-headed men who were talking energetically.

"I agree that there's a lot to be said for Gandhi, but there's more to be said for Tagore," the more tousled of the two men was saying.

Daddyji's dormant nationalist sentiments were stirred up. "Tagore is a bloodsucking Bengali landlord," he broke in. "A stooge of the British. That's how he originally got his knighthood."

La Touche, who was standing next to Daddyji, pinched his arm and quickly drew him aside. "Do you realize who it was that you just contradicted?" La Touche whispered. "A great friend of Tagore, our poet W. B. Yeats." They rejoined the circle, and La Touche introduced the now sheepish Daddyji to Yeats and his interlocutor, Bertrand Russell.

Back in London, Daddyji received a long, tearful, almost incoherent letter from Daulat Ram. "We were shocked to hear that you do not want to return home," he said. "I would have kept the news from Bhabiji, but, sadly, I was out when your hopeless letter came, and Balwant read it to her. Since then, she hasn't slept, and she weeps all day long. She has developed palpitations, and the doctor says no medicine can really help her, for she is grieving. If something happens to her, don't blame me afterward for not telling you how things were. Whenever I see her, I have to leave abruptly and go and cry by myself—it's so heart-rending. What is London, what is worldly success, what is money, compared to Bhabiji, and her love for her son and heir? Come home at once."

Daddyji knew he had to go back.

VII

PATERFAMILIAS

A FTER LALAJI DIED, BHABIJI, DAULAT RAM, AND THE children continued to live for a time in the house that Lalaji had rented when the family moved to Lahore. It was next door to the Arya Samaj high school, and the whole neighborhood had a devotional, studious air. Daulat Ram, who had remained a villager at heart, felt comfortable in this atmosphere and was also glad of the steadying influence of the Arya Samaj on the growing children. Balwant and Raj Kanwar, Lalaji's third and fourth sons, and Jaswant, their first cousin, were highspirited and excelled in sports at Government College, and the house had the additional advantage of being near the college playing fields. After a few months, however, Daulat Ram was befriended by a Mr. Iqbal (his identity has been disguised), a Punjabi with a winning manner who was a local landlord. He lived in a large house in Little Lane, not far from the Mall, the most fashionable road in Lahore. He could not afford the upkeep of the house, and he invited Daulat Ram to share the house and the rent with him.

Mr. Iqbal's residence was more than two miles from Government College, but because Daulat Ram saw in Mr. Iqbal's offer a chance to better the family's situation, the family moved into one half of the large house, and Mr. Iqbal and his young, pregnant wife retired to the other half. It soon became apparent that the new neighborhood was hedged in by *gullis* of courtesans and of nautch and singing girls, and that Mr.

Iqbal was notorious in the local bazaar for not paying
for the things he bought; he owned the land on which
the bazaar stood, and no one there dared collect from
the landlord. Moreover, he enjoyed the company of
unsavory characters, whom he entertained regularly at
rowdy parties. But once Daulat Ram had made the
move, he had little choice but to keep the family to his
side of the house and ignore the goings on in Mr. Iqbal's
quarters. Anyway, Daulat Ram was an earnest man
of simple habits, and accepted Mr. Iqbal's excesses as
private vagaries. Not so Balwant, Jaswant, and Raj
Kanwar, who shared a room with a window looking
out onto the street and onto Mr. Iqbal's front door. At
dusk, when they were supposed to be doing their homework, they would stand at the window and watch men
arriving in twos and threes, slapping one another on
the back and swaggering through Mr. Iqbal's doorway.
The boys would listen for familiar sounds from the
other side of the house—shouts of greeting and calls for
drinks, explosions of laughter and the clatter of poker
chips. Later, when it was dark, and the three were in
bed, they would hear the clink of glass bangles and the
shuffle of sandals in the street, the unbolting and bolting
of the door, and the tuning up of instruments. There
would be the tap-tap of a hammer on the tabla pegs, the
swelling and subsiding of a harmonium note, answered
by the whine of the sarangi as its string was tightened
to the harmonium's pitch. Music would drift into the
boys' room—waterfalls of melody, jingling ankle bells,
thudding heels, a childlike voice singing, "I am your—
your very own—goldfinch."

Balwant, Jaswant, and Raj Kanwar had been average students, known from the start of their college careers mainly for high living and physical prowess. Balwant was tough, wiry, and friendly, and was the captain of the college swimming team. Raj Kanwar stood six feet tall, had powerful limbs and a forbidding look, and was the best football player in the college. He had the kick of a horse and the tackle of a python. As for Jaswant, he tagged along with them. The three were all known as "muscle men," and had founded a student gang called the Invincibles, which practiced wrestling, boxing, and intimidation, and offered protection from rival gangs. The Invincibles made their headquarters near Government College, at the shop of a tailor who liked the company of students and was always eager to get together a group for poker in the back part of his shop, which he had stocked with soft drinks, *pan*, and *biris* (hand-rolled cigarettes). In fact, Balwant, Jaswant, and Raj Kanwar came to regard the shop as a more accessible version of Mr. Iqbal's revels, to which they knew they could not as yet aspire. Instead of attending classes, they would while away entire days in the tailor's company, reporting on their imaginary conquests, telling off-color stories, drinking bottled lemonade, choking on *pan*, and playing cards for high stakes. They felt important and worldly, and were rarely wanting for money; it arrived in the house regularly from Daddyji and Daulat Ram, and Bhabiji never begrudged them any of it—and they took full advantage of her liberality. Now and again, the tailor would remember his business and put his young cronies to work, getting the day's labor done in a couple of hours. Balwant shone as a cutter; he had a steady hand with the scissors and a good eye for patterns. The boys came to think that if they failed to get their degrees Balwant could always earn his living as a tailor, with Jaswant and Raj Kanwar rounding up customers.

As it turned out, Balwant, who was the first one up, did fail the examination for the degree of Bachelor of Science. A year later, he sat for the examination again, this time with Jaswant and Raj Kanwar. All three were certain that they had failed, and when the tailor came to know of it, he introduced Balwant to a clever barber who had recently earned notoriety by claiming that it was within his power to get anyone passed. The barber, who went daily to the home of the college registrar to give him a shave, let it be known that in this way he had become the registrar's confidant, and that if he whispered a student's name in the registrar's ear, the registrar passed the student—provided the barber discreetly left a few hundred-rupee notes under the shaving mug. The barber said that he asked no commission for himself—the good deed was its own reward. When Balwant heard about this intrigue, he was skeptical, and said as much to the barber. The barber replied, "You can come and see for yourself how I stand with the Registrar Sahib." The barber took Balwant to the registrar's house and hid him on the veranda, behind a *chik* (bamboo blind). Balwant watched while the barber set about preparing a chair on the veranda, calling to a servant for hot water, shaking out a smock, getting out his implements, and stropping his razor. Presently, the registrar came out in his dressing gown and bare feet, nodded to the barber, and sat down in the chair. As the barber applied lather to the registrar's face, he chattered volubly. Although Balwant was not able to make out what the barber was saying, he saw the registrar's high-bridged nose frequently wrinkle up. Balwant took this to be a gesture of approval. Again, although he did not see any sign of money, he was persuaded beyond doubt that the two men were on such intimate terms that the barber must be the registrar's cat's-paw. Balwant quietly slipped away, went straight to Bhabiji, and, pleading a life-or-death emergency, got her to give him five hundred rupees—most of her savings—which he then took to the barber to give to the registrar on behalf of Jaswant, Raj Kanwar, and himself.

AT ABOUT THE TIME that Balwant was sealing his bargain with the barber, Daddyji arrived in Bombay from England. Before proceeding to Lahore, he stopped off in Delhi. He had heard that Chhoti Bhabiji was there just then, in Lady Harding Medical College Hospital, recovering from a hysterectomy. (She had had thirteen miscarriages and stillbirths, and had never succeeded in having a child.) He went straight to her hospital room to see her. He had not heard from her or Bhaji Ganga Ram since the Rawalpindi days, even though, following Lalaji's death, he had written to Bhaji Ganga Ram from New York, saying that now that Lalaji was gone, Bhaji Ganga Ram was the most respected member of the clan, and they all looked to him for guidance. In Delhi, Daddyji went up to Bhaji Ganga Ram, who was sitting at Chhoti Bhabiji's bedside—older, thinner, grayer, but holding himself very straight—and placed at his feet a Decca gramophone he had brought for them from London.

Bhaji Ganga Ram looked at him and then at the machine, and broke into a hesitant smile. He stood up, Chhoti Bhabiji blessed Daddyji from her bed, and the uncle and nephew embraced.

When Daddyji reached Lahore—Bhabiji could scarcely believe that her first-born son had actually returned—he got wind of what Balwant, Jaswant, and Raj Kanwar had been up to. He berated Daulat Ram for not keeping a watchful eye and a tight rein on his younger brothers, and for allowing himself to be trapped in the unhealthy atmosphere of Mr. Iqbal's house. As it happened, Mr. Iqbal was convicted just at that time of bribing government officers and was imprisoned. Daddyji arranged to keep Mr. Iqbal's house for Bhabiji, and he and Daulat Ram agreed to contribute half of whatever they earned to its maintenance until every last child had completed his education. (Years later, Daddyji came across Mr. Iqbal in Amritsar. He was giving a discourse on the Gita and the *puranas* at a Hindu temple, of which he was custodian. Though he had grown an impressive beard and mustache, his voice betrayed him, as did the way he glanced at the women in the audience.)

Daddyji next confronted the three boys, and told them that they had been living in a fool's paradise. He was going to see to it, he said, that they set about fulfilling Lalaji's wish that each of his sons should have a college degree, a bungalow, and a motorcar.

They apologized, and told him not to worry, because the barber would fix everything.

Daddyji extracted the full story, and then demanded, "Do you really think that anyone can bribe his way to a degree? That a mere barber can have influence on a registrar? Have you all taken leave of your senses?"

Balwant swore that after giving the money to the barber he had received "personal assurances from the registrar's own lips" that the results had been duly fixed.

Daddyji didn't believe Balwant, and asked to be taken to the registrar, but Balwant begged him to let well enough alone, and Daddyji, thinking that the boys would learn their lesson soon enough, let the matter rest.

Just as Daddyji had feared, Balwant, Jaswant, and Raj Kanwar all failed.

Daddyji remonstrated with the three boys. He tried to get them to sit for the examination again. Raj Kanwar agreed. Jaswant adamantly refused, and Daddyji eventually got him appointed superintendent of a district tribal settlement. As for Balwant, he replied, "My middle name is happy-go-lucky. My *biris* are my books. A failed B.Sc. is distinction enough for me. I'm the sort of man on whom fortune smiles. You'll see—I'll win a big lottery and buy you all motorcars and bungalows." He entreated Daddyji to apprentice him to his friend the tailor, and Daddyji did. Balwant, on his own, enrolled in a correspondence course in tailoring offered by a trade school in London. After a year, he received the diploma of a master cutter.

DADDYJI, a month after his return from abroad, got an appointment, with good prospects for promotion, in the new Public Health Department of the Punjab. He was sent to Murree, a small hill station above Rawalpindi, to fight a spreading cholera epidemic, and when it abated, he was posted as district health officer to Montgomery, the headquarters of a new district, formed after the excavation of the Lower Bari Doab Canal. He rode out to Montgomery on a motorcycle he had brought back from England. The station was an open place, with a country atmosphere. It had plenty of fertile land, thanks to the even supply of canal water; moreover, there were large fruit and vegetable farms and also breeding farms for cows, sheep, camels, and horses, all subsidized by the government to build up the new district.

To have time to look for a place of his own in Montgomery, Daddyji put up in the local dak bungalow, by the canal. The day after he arrived, he ran across an old friend of Bhaji Ganga Ram's named Vidyadhar at the Montgomery Club. "My wife and children have escaped to the hills from this infernal summer heat," Vidyadhar said. "Move in with me, and we can be merry bachelors together."

"I couldn't think of imposing on you in that way," Daddyji said.

"You're England-returned, America-returned, and you've never heard of paying guests?" Vidyadhar asked. "Of course, we'll share expenses—go fifty-fifty."

Now, it turned out that Vidyadhar was a tippler, while Daddyji, being a total abstainer, was content to sip hot milk from the traditional brass tumbler. When they had been living together for two weeks, they sat down to settle accounts. Daddyji was horrified to see whiskey on the household bills and to realize that he was subsidizing such a heinous habit. "You look as if someone had hit you over the head," Vidyadhar said to him. "As long as you don't insist that I pay for your milk, I won't insist on your paying for my whiskey." Vidyadhar was a sterling fellow after all, Daddyji thought, and he blamed himself for ever thinking otherwise.

When Vidyadhar's family returned, at the beginning of winter, Daddyji moved into a bungalow of his own. Now that he had not only a motor-driven conveyance and a job but also a bungalow, he had to start thinking of a wife. Daulat Ram had just got married— he had taken his wife, Subhadran, to Rawalpindi, where he was posted as a district health officer in the new Public Health Department—and the fact that the older brother, senior to him in the department, was still unmarried was causing some talk among the relatives. They were free with speculations. "He has a girl waiting for him in England," they said, and "He's looking for a girl with a big dowry," and "Maybe there's something wrong with him."

Daddyji was in great demand in the marriage market, and there were many proposals. (Some arrived by post and others through go-betweens.) He discussed them with a neighbor, a worldly senior advocate, who had two marriageable sons, and who kept wall charts in his bedroom on which he listed, in parallel columns, the assets and liabilities of each proposal: the extent of the girl's education, the size of her dowry, the reputation of her family, and her appearance. Each proposal was recorded under the date of its receipt, with the tabulation of its desirability. The advocate advised Daddyji to adopt this system of wall charts, saying he was certain to come to grief otherwise, but Daddyji could not bring himself to tot up the assets and liabilities of his proposals in such a manner.

One day, a superintending engineer in the Public Works Department arrived on Daddyji's doorstep and launched immediately into a catalogue of his daughter's good points. "She is convent-educated and speaks English like a memsahib," he said. "She is a B.A. and a talented bridge player. She has fair skin, thick hair, and clear features, and she looks well fed."

Daddyji was all attention until the superintending engineer brought out her photograph. Then, without further thought, Daddyji dismissed the proposal. She wore spectacles.

That evening, at the Montgomery Club, when Daddyji was telling about his narrow escape, someone asked him, "What are your demands in respect to a dowry?"

"I am self-supporting and an idealist," Daddyji said. "My wife should be her own dowry. She should be presentable, she should be fluent in English, and she should be musical. I would like her to be able to give good parties, and sing and play the harmonium for my guests. I want her to be modern and free of superstitions. I would, of course, like her to come to my clubs with me, and be able to walk and talk with the Indian and English wives."

A few days later, Mr. Khan Chand, a senior sub-

Mamaji, Proposal Portrait, 1925

judge, who had overheard Daddyji at the club, accosted him and said, "I think I've found you a wife." He held out two pictures of a girl. In one she was standing and in the other she was sitting. She had large, serious, dark eyes in a soft, innocent, intelligent face; a womanly body; and long, thick hair. "She's the daughter of Lala Durga Das Mehra," Khan Chand was saying. "You must have heard of him. He's a famous Arya Samajist of Lahore. He's a senior advocate on the Punjab High Court, a member of the Syndicate of Punjab University, and president of the Dayanand Anglo-Vernacular College Management and Trust Society. I was just in Lahore as his guest. What do you think of her?"

"She's beautiful and fetching," Daddyji said.

Daddyji went to Lahore on one of his visits. When he had finished a game of tennis at the Engineering Club, he was approached by two prominent Arya Samajists—friends of Bhaji Ganga Ram and, by coincidence, of Lala Durga Das Mehra—who had been waiting to see him.

"We know the kind of girl you've been looking for, and Lala Durga Das's daughter is just the girl for you," one of them said.

"She meets all your specifications," the other Arya Samajist said. "We hear she is highly educated and accomplished in music, and she's well versed in household duties."

"She's the eldest girl among seven children and knows everything about looking after young ones," the first Arya Samajist said.

That very night, Daddyji wrote to Bhaji Ganga Ram, dwelling on the girl's beauty and education, extolling her Arya Samaj upbringing, which insured freedom from superstition, and asking for Bhaji Ganga Ram's permission to marry her. He received a letter from Bhaji Ganga Ram by return post, giving his blessing.

The first thing that Bhabiji did after she heard the news of Daddyji's intentions was to go with Bibi Parmeshwari Devi to Lala Durga Das's house for the viewing and reservation ceremony. They reported that the girl was seventeen but fully mature. She was shy and respectful, and would fit into the family very well. They had fixed the wedding date for the seventh of December. It was 1925.

Daddyji, being anxious to see his bride himself, got on his motorcycle and rode to Lala Durga Das's house, a dark little building just outside the Shahalmi Gate of the native city. He stood watch, shooing away throngs of urchins who wanted to touch the magical machine. After a couple of hours, two young women, their heads and faces veiled, came out of the house and quickly got into a waiting carriage. Daddyji was sure that one of them was his bride, and chased after them, somehow managing, in spite of the crowds, to bring his motorcycle alongside and peer into the carriage, but all he could see was fluttering veils.

DADDYJI's prospective father-in-law informed Bhabiji that his Kshatriya caste group had decided to keep the ceremonial functions of marriages to a minimum. Anyhow, he had three other daughters to marry off and did not want to set an expensive precedent. "Economy is a necessity, but austerity is a virtue," he said. He hoped, therefore, that Bhabiji would not mind if he restricted the usual three- or four-day marriage festivities to the wedding day itself. Bhabiji, of course, deferred to his wishes.

On the evening before the religious ceremony, as Daddyji was mounting a hired wedding horse for the customary journey to the bride's house, the members of his wedding party gathered around him, grumbling at the meagreness of the arrangements. These were all close relatives, many of whom had come from Nawankote or Burkhurdar for the occasion. They complained about not having been shaved, trimmed, dressed, and fêted for several days previously by the bride's parents. Nor had they been able to go over the dowry, item by item, appraising its worth and magnificence; in place of jewelry and finery, the bride's parents had bought Daddyji a 1924 demonstration-model Chevrolet. So as not to overshadow the arrangements in the bride's house, the bridegroom's relatives were barred from accompanying him in a wedding procession, the silver and gold ornaments on the wedding horse had been kept as simple as possible, and the brass band that ordinarily serenaded the bridegroom with love songs as he rode was missing. Daddyji was to ride alone to his bride's house for an overnight stay under the roof of his prospective father-in-law.

Daddyji told his disappointed relatives that the wishes of the bride's parents had to be honored, and boldly clopped away, ignoring the chill of the wintry evening.

At the bride's house, Daddyji was put to bed in the

guest room. He was awakened at five o'clock in the morning, and he quickly bathed and put on clean clothes and went out to the inner courtyard, where a wedding canopy had been set up. Beneath it, on colorful pallets and cushions around a sacred fire, sat Bhabiji and his closest relatives and the bride and her closest relatives. The Brahman performing the ceremony seated Daddyji on a wooden board alongside the bride.

Toward the end of the two-hour ceremony, the Brahman asked Daddyji, "How do you name this child?"

Daddyji looked at the veiled and bedecked apparition, whose face he had not seen and whose voice he had not heard. "What *is* her name?" he asked.

He heard a jumble of voices from the congregation of wedding guests.

"You're supposed to give her a name!"

"Now!"

"He doesn't know!"

The Brahman said, "Her old name is Shanti Devi."

"I like that name very much, thank you," said Daddyji. "I'll keep it."

After the marriage rites and the wedding breakfast, the bride was put in a palanquin and carried to Bhabiji's house for an overnight stay with Daddyji. Then she was returned to her parents for a few days, and Daddyji drove back to Montgomery in his new car. As soon as he reached home, he sat down and wrote her his first letter. It was in English, and it was long and extremely adulatory. He said how beautiful she was and how charming she was. He thought she was the sweetest person he had ever met. He had travelled as far as

Richmond, Virginia, and he knew that there was no one like her anywhere. He said his only regret was that in the short time they had been together he had hardly heard her speak, let alone sing, as he had hoped to hear her do. But he was consoled by the fact that they had their entire lives ahead of them, and that he would be hearing her sing often. She must be sure to bring her harmonium to Montgomery with her.

Daddyji sealed the envelope, posted the letter himself, and waited for a reply, wondering what her handwriting would be like, what she would say. He imagined she would write in girlish convent English. One day went by, then two days, three, four, and five; still there was no reply. His letter must have gone astray.

He wrote a second letter. If anything, it was longer and more admiring than the first.

Eventually, he received a few lines back from her, saying, in simple Hindi, that she could not read or understand English—though she had been taught some English words in preparation for her marriage. She said that she had studied Hindi at school, but that when she failed an examination in geography a few years earlier her father had taken her out of school, saying, "You're not fit for books. You should keep to cooking, washing, and looking after your younger brothers and sisters."

Daddyji read and reread her letter. It couldn't possibly be meant for him. She couldn't possibly be his wife. Her letter was the first intimation he had had that his father-in-law was perhaps less of an educationalist in private than he was in public. Was it possible that the two Arya Samajists had taken advantage of Daddyji's gullibility? Or had they themselves been misled? Perhaps his father-in-law had not been told of his demands. Daddyji would never know. He wondered what she would do at a club. How would she mix? At least, she was true to her photographs.

A couple of days after Mamaji (the name by which she has always been known to us children) arrived in Montgomery, Mrs. Vidyadhar gave a party for her and Daddyji, to which everyone in the community of government officers—the high society of Montgomery —was invited. Mamaji and Daddyji drove over to the Vidyadhars', and as soon as they arrived, Mamaji was taken to one room for dinner and simple rummy with the ladies, and Daddyji to another room for dinner and bridge with the men. When the time came to leave, Daddyji went to the room where the ladies were, and looked around for Mamaji among the groups seated at the card tables. He didn't see her.

"Where is my good wife?" he asked Mrs. Vidyadhar.

Everyone giggled.

Mrs. Vidyadhar pointed out a girl sitting just in front of him. It was Mamaji. She looked confused, and much younger than her years; she had come wearing a sari of Benares silk, with her hair in a matronly chignon, but she now had on Punjabi trousers, a tunic-like knee-length shirt, and a cardigan, and her hair was hanging down her back in a girlish plait.

"So you can't even recognize your own wife," Mrs. Vidyadhar said jokingly. "That's what happens when you men get together and drink yourselves under the table."

Daddyji laughed along with the ladies, thinking that perhaps it would be just as well to wait until he and Mamaji got home before he asked her about her change of clothes.

Daddyji and Mamaji got into the front seat of the car, and Harish Chander, the Montgomery postmaster, and his wife, Tara, who were being given a lift, got into the back seat. The car was wedged in so tightly between two other cars that Daddyji had to back out at an awkward angle, and his right rear wheel went through a hedge.

Tara, carrying on Mrs. Vidyadhar's joke, said, "I've always said that tipsy men are a menace to hedges and to us poor ladies. If you value your life and your dowry, Shanti, you'll get him to keep a driver."

Daddyji laughed, but when, after dropping Harish and Tara off, they reached home, he noticed that Mamaji was trembling all over. "What's the matter?" he asked.

"Please don't beat me!" she cried out.

"Beat you?"

"They beat them."

"Who beat whom?"

"My mother warned me—all drunkards beat their wives."

Daddyji was getting angry. The joke had gone far enough. But he remembered that Manji used to say that drunkards beat their wives, and he said to Mamaji mildly, "I've never touched a drop of liquor."

"Then how is it that you don't recognize your own wife?"

"What ever did you change your clothes for?"

"Mrs. Vidyadhar insisted," Mamaji said. "She said I would catch cold."

It was some time before Daddyji could explain to Mamaji's satisfaction that Mrs. Vidyadhar and Tara had been joking.

As Daddyji had asked, Mamaji had brought a small hand harmonium—a brand-new one—to Montgomery with her, but it was days before he could get her to sit down with it. Then, instead of playing the instrument, she held one key down, squeezed the bellows in a gingerly way, and looked frightened at the quavering sound of the note, which seemed to start up and die down as if it had a will of its own.

While Daddyji watched and clapped in encouragement, she raised her thin voice in a discordant hymn. Then she faltered, stopped, and broke down. Through her tears, she said that she had received no instruction in music.

So! She had no more knowledge of music than she had of English! But what had happened had happened. Perhaps it was too late to instruct her in English, but he would certainly give her some lessons in music.

Every evening thereafter, Daddyji—who had had no instruction in music, either—would sit with Mamaji on the floor and try to teach her how to pump the harmonium to achieve a steady tone, and how to strengthen her voice by singing simple scales. But she seemed to be tone-deaf, and one day Daddyji, in complete exasperation, flung the harmonium across the room, and the subject of music was never mentioned again.

Daddyji went for a ride on his English motorcycle one afternoon. He had an old sweater on his lap, and somehow the sweater got tangled up in the motorcycle chain and became torn and stained with grease. When he got home, he took the sweater to the bedroom, where Mamaji was sitting on her charpoy with an embroidery frame in her lap while the punka wallah (there was no electricity in the house) sat at the foot of the bed pulling the punka cord and making the fan overhead creak and swing back and forth drowsily, barely stirring the sultry air.

Daddyji held out the sweater. "I have a riddle for you," he said to her, in a teasing way. "If you can guess how this sweater got torn, I will give you a trip to England one day."

She examined the sweater closely.

"The clue is in the stains," he said.

A baffled expression came over her face, changing to one of pain.

"Motorcycle," he said, and, seeing her anguish, he added quickly, "But I'd made up my mind to give you a trip to England long ago anyway." He gave her his hand to seal the promise, and she broke into a slow smile.

Mamaji was observant and ready to learn, and she liked to be indulged, but although she carried herself like a maharani, she lacked self-confidence. She had led a cloistered life within the walls of her father's house. When she needed a pair of shoes, her father's *munshi* (clerk) had been sent out and had come back with a trunkful of shoes of various sizes and designs, which she tried on in the privacy of the ladies' quarters. She had kept one pair, and the *munshi* had returned the rest of the shoes. She had not once been inside a shop.

The first time Mamaji and Daddyji went to Lahore together—they drove there and back nearly every weekend—Daddyji parked his car right outside the most fashionable bazaar in the Punjab, named Anarkali, after a sixteenth-century Muslim courtesan. He led the way into the narrow, bright, crowded street of open shops, and she followed, trying not to look to either side. She was at once reluctant and eager, paralyzed and thrilled.

A few steps inside Anarkali, there was a new shoe shop, run by a well-respected Kshatriya gentleman, a Master of Arts from Punjab University, who was something of a pioneer. His shop had a signboard reading, "*B.A. bane lohar to M.A. chamar ho,/ Phir dekhiye bahar keh kaisi bahar ho*" ("When a B.A. becomes a blacksmith and an M.A. becomes a tanner, then let's see how the country flourishes"). Not only was it unusual for someone with a university degree to take up shopkeeping but among Hindus anyone who handled skins or leather for a living was considered an Untouchable.

Daddyji slipped some rupee notes into Mamaji's hand and took her into the shop. She tried on practically everything before she settled on a pair of high-heeled gold sandals. They were her first purchase.

Daddyji's work at Montgomery was spread all over the district, a rural area studded with old and new villages, and he had to go on longish tours to oversee vaccinations against the triple terrors of plague, cholera, and smallpox. Mamaji accompanied him on the tours, and when he went on an inspection she would stay in the rest house they were stopping at, and while away the time in the garden, picking sweet peas or acacia blooms, or gathering lemons or oranges. Once, when they were staying at Okara, they went for a morning walk together. It was a very hot day, and when they came to a canal, Daddyji dived in. He surfaced, swam to the opposite bank, and looked back at her. She stood stupefied. It came to him that not only had she never been in the water in her life but also she had no idea that anyone could swim in it.

From that day on, whenever it was practicable, he gave her swimming lessons, and although her progress was slow, in time she did get over her fear of water.

Near Daddyji's bungalow in Montgomery were an open stretch of road and a field; Daddyji took Mamaji there in the car one day and pointed out the steering wheel, the pedals, and the gearshift, and some knobs on the dashboard. He said, "Turn this. . . . Pull this to start. . . . Step on this, and pull this toward you to go up a hill."

She listened to him attentively and did what he told her.

He took her out driving several times, and then said, "You should drive out by yourself. Why don't you take Tara and Mrs. Vidyadhar up the canal bank for a picnic lunch?" He invited them for her, and on the appointed day he cranked the car up and saw them off.

As the car wobbled down the gravel drive, with all three ladies dressed in their best gold-embroidered saris, he saw Mamaji's hand leave the steering wheel for a moment and wave to him bravely. Then they were gone in a cloud of dust.

He felt happy, and pleased with his success as a teacher. He went inside and tried to do some paperwork but was unable to concentrate. He kept listening for the rasp of tires on gravel—he was eager to hear the details of the outing—but instead, a few hours later, he heard stealthy little footsteps on the veranda, and he went out.

There was Mamaji, her face flushed and perspiring.

"The car?" Daddyji asked. "Where are Tara and Mrs. Vidyadhar? Are they hurt?"

She shook her head.

"The car—is it in the canal?"

She shook her head.

He couldn't get her to say anything for some time. Eventually, she brought out the words "The car is broken."

Daddyji found the car up the road. It was out of petrol. He realized his mistake—he had never told her what made the car run.

Daddyji and Mamaji had been married more than two months, and Mamaji had still not conceived. She and her mother feared the worst. Her mother made Daddyji take Mamaji to the leading gynecologist in Lahore, a middle-aged woman; her diagnosis was that Mamaji had an infantile uterus and was incapable of having children.

When they returned from the doctor's office, Mamaji clasped her hands and said, "Do with me what you like, but *don't* send me back to my parents."

"What are you talking about?"

She said she knew that a woman was like a pair of

shoes—when she wasn't useful a man threw her away and got another.

"Such customs may be prevalent among city people, but we are country people," Daddyji said angrily. "For us, a woman is not a pair of shoes but a goddess. Once married, always married."

"Please take a second wife," she begged. "I will stay in the house and be a sister to her, and look after your children."

"That may be the practice among city people, but not among us country people," he said.

"But we Hindu women are like breeding cows," she said, between her sobs. "Our value is in our sons."

Daddyji pointed to the example of Bhaji Ganga Ram and Chhoti Bhabiji. "Look at them. Bhaji Ganga Ram has been married to her for twenty-five years, and she is childless. Has he taken another wife? You're going to be my one and only wife, and my younger brothers will be our children."

He told her that women often didn't conceive for years, but she was inconsolable, and he took her to another gynecologist for a second opinion. The new diagnosis was that Mamaji's uterus only appeared to be infantile because it was retroflexed. The gynecologist showed Mamaji how to lie on her stomach and do knee-elbow exercises, and said that in time Mamaji should be able to conceive. And right away she did.

Mamaji and Daddyji threw themselves into the planning and building of a house in Montgomery. With a loan, Daddyji bought a one-and-a-half-acre triangular plot of land in the middle of the community of government officers, and he got hold of a handbook of architecture giving plans and elevations for various kinds of houses. After Daddyji had studied it and Mamaji had looked at the drawings, they chose the design. Like a typical canal rest house, it was to be airy and well ventilated, with a central hall running from a front veranda to a back veranda, and, opening off it, four large, high-ceilinged rooms.

One fine day, they moved into the new house, and there they waited for the baby to arrive. Daddyji planted a lawn and put in a tennis court second to none in the British or Indian clubs in the district; Mamaji bought seedlings and slips from the farms and planted them all around the lawn, and enjoyed walking in the garden and watching the plants blossom. Almost a year after they were married, Mamaji gave birth to a baby girl, and they named her Promila.

It happened that Daddyji's immediate superior, Dr. Abdul Rehman, the assistant director of public health, was a bridge addict. He was famous in the department for his hospitable nature, and for his flouting of Muslim taboos: he had a seemingly inexhaustible capacity for whiskey, which he always took with a little soda and without ice. Whenever he came from Lahore to Montgomery, the local civil surgeon, Dr. Nazir Hussain, arranged a bridge party for him. Daddyji was often invited to join in, but for the most part stayed away, fearing cards as he would a dangerous temptress. But he, Dr. Rehman, and Dr. Hussain often had to tour the district together, and during these tours, when they put up in rest houses, Daddyji, along with any local officer who happened to be available, was roped into a bridge game. Daddyji was in no position to refuse, because Dr.

Mamaji, Daddyji, and Promila, Montgomery, 1926

Rehman's recommendation was necessary for a permanent post in the department.

Daddyji studied a few books on bridge, and soon found that Dr. Rehman was no match for him. He began winning consistently, and even though Dr. Rehman conveniently forgot to pay his losses—a matter that his subordinate was too tactful to call to his attention—Daddyji still came out ahead every month. Dr. Rehman liked the arrangement so well that he found excuses to make special tours in the district, and Daddyji, for his part, became so intoxicated with his new-found talent that he came to think of the bridge table as a home away from home.

VIII

CAREER

T HE DREAM OF DADDYJI'S STUDENT DAYS HAD BEEN to live and work in Lahore, and three years after his marriage he was transferred there, having been made a permanent member of the department some time before. He sold his house in Montgomery and bought a plot of land on Temple Road. It was in the best section of Lahore, about a quarter of a mile from Lawrence Gardens, the huge park lying along the Mall. On the Mall were European-type shops, the cathedral, and the museum celebrated in "Kim" (John Lockwood Kipling, Rudyard's father, had been its director), and the Gardens themselves contained an extensive botanical section, a menagerie, cricket grounds, and private clubs. Just beyond the Gardens lay the racecourse. On the Temple Road land, Daddyji built a house, which was three stories high and was made of bricks and cement. In front of the house was a little lawn and in back was an enclosed courtyard; alongside was a narrow driveway leading to the garage, over which Daddyji put some extra rooms, as a sort of annex. Most important of all, the house had electricity and running water. As soon as it was completed, Daddyji, Mamaji, and their two daughters—Promila had been followed by Nirmila—moved in, and so did all the other members of the family living in Lahore. A third daughter, Urmila, who arrived soon afterward, was the first baby born in the new house.

Daddyji, however, spent little time at home. After work, he would get into his new car, a 1928 Model A

Ford, which was a successor to the dowry Chevrolet, and drive along the Mall and around Lawrence Gardens, or up the hill road, on which he had bicycled so often in his student days. He would park on the hilltop and gaze at the façade of Government College and then coast down to the Punjab Association Club, a modest society exclusively for Indians, where he would play bridge with none other than the redoubtable Saleem, who was still tennis singles champion, and who still divided his time between Lahore and London. Daddyji had made such progress in bridge that club members began to bet on him as they would on a racehorse.

Aside from cards, what Daddyji liked most about club life was the repartee. Saleem was the undefeated master of the quick riposte until one day early in the new year when Kanwar Dalip Singh, a distinguished barrister known for his prowess as a hunter, walked into the card room. Everyone greeted him and wished him a happy New Year.

"I understand, Kanwar Sahib, that you were shooting tigers over the Christmas holidays," Saleem said, looking up from his cards. Everyone waited to see what he was up to.

"That's right, Saleem. Not much luck, though," Kanwar Sahib replied.

"I hope you met a jackal, at least," Saleem said dryly. He went back to his cards with an air of self-satisfaction.

He got the expected titters around the table at the notion of the brave hunter going after the cowardly jackal, but then Kanwar Sahib laid his hand on Saleem's shoulder and said, in the most fatherly tone he could summon, "Yes, Saleem, I did, and he said, 'Please remember me to my dear brother Saleem.'" It was the only time anyone in the club had seen Saleem bested at anything, and he never lived it down.

The clubs within Lawrence Gardens were the Lahore Gymkhana Club, for the Europeans, and the Cosmopolitan Club, a grander version of the Punjab Association Club, for the Indians—each with its own tennis courts. One day, Daddyji was at the courts of the Gymkhana Club, as a guest, watching Saleem—he was an exception in being a member—play in the North India Tennis Tournament. What long legs he had, and what big hands! His service could be better, but his strategy was perfect. He was playing from the baseline, smashing the ball back with a top spin and letting his opponent make all the mistakes.

After the match, Saleem introduced Daddyji to a Mr. Puckle, captain of the Gymkhana Club cricket team. "I took up cricket in a serious way a few years ago, when I was posted in Rawalpindi," Daddyji said to Mr. Puckle. "I had a supervisor under me who was one of the best bowlers in the Punjab. On Saturday afternoons and Sunday mornings, he used to give me a lot of practice in the nets at the Pindi Club, and with his coaching I became a tolerable batsman."

"Why don't you come to our nets and practice with us?" said Mr. Puckle.

Soon after this, Mr. Puckle got Daddyji elected to the Gymkhana Club. He and Saleem were among only half a dozen Indian members.

From then on, Daddyji was seen even less around the house, because every weekend he played cricket for the Gymkhana Club against one of the colleges or one of the other clubs. Once, he rated a banner headline in the *Civil & Military Gazette:* "THREE BRILLIANT CATCHES BY MEHTA."

After three years in Lahore, Daddyji took a leave of absence from his department and went to Delhi to work for the King George Thanksgiving (Anti-Tuberculosis) Fund Committee, established to solicit contributions in honor of the King-Emperor, who not long before had come down with such a severe case of pleurisy that doctors were afraid it might develop into tuberculosis. King George's chest had eventually cleared up, and to mark his restoration to health Lord Irwin, the Viceroy of India, had made an appeal for a Thanksgiving Fund. Subscribed to by the native princes, among others, it was designated for publicity and propaganda against tuberculosis, and placed in the hands of a subcommittee of the Red Cross Society. Daddyji was appointed the subcommittee's organizing secretary.

When Daddyji was not touring the British provinces and princely states to set up local anti-tuberculosis committees, he and Mamaji lived in New Delhi, the winter capital, or in Simla, the summer capital. Being tall, handsome, courtly, and athletic, he was quickly accepted into the social circles of both capitals; in Simla he played in invitational tennis tournaments at the Viceregal Lodge, and in New Delhi he was invited to viceregal receptions and to dinners given by maharajas. Now and again, however, he got into difficulties with less Westernized Indians. He was a member of the executive committee of the Chelmsford Club—named for Viscount Chelmsford, a former viceroy. During one meeting, in Simla, the recurrent topic of the club's finances came up yet again. "The club maintains buildings and grounds both in Simla and in Delhi, yet we hardly ever make use of our Simla facilities," said Sir Fazli Husain, who was presiding over the meeting. He was chairman of the Fund subcommittee, a viceregal executive councillor, and a devout Muslim. "It has been suggested that we close down our Simla establishment altogether, to save operating expenses. I must say I agree."

"I agree with the suggestion, Sir Fazli," said Daddyji. "But, if I may, I would like to put forward a qualification—that we keep the club alive in Simla by renting space in the Cecil Hotel. My friends and I have done some legwork, and we have discovered that we can rent a couple of rooms there very reasonably."

"It would be very derogatory to associate the name of the Viceroy with a hotel," Sir Fazli said.

"Sir, it would be still more derogatory to the Viceroy to close down the club in Simla entirely," Daddyji rejoined.

Sir Fazli was visibly ruffled, but he said only, "The deliberation of this question shall be postponed to the agenda of the next meeting."

Outside the club, as Sir Fazli was preparing to leave in a rickshaw, he said to Daddyji, "Dr. Mehta, I expected more tact from you than you exhibited in the meeting today."

Daddyji, remembering a saying of Lalaji's—"Never corner a tiger without leaving him room to escape"—quickly replied, "Sir, it was only in the interests of the club that I spoke."

"Even in the club, I remain a viceregal executive councillor," Sir Fazli said sternly. "As an Indian, you must not imitate the English clubmen, who take liberties with one another, even address the governor of the province by his first name—nay, drink and tell smutty stories."

Daddyji apologized profusely for his tactlessness.

Sir Fazli waited to hear him out, then shouted to the rickshaw coolies, "Home!" The rickshaw shot away.

One of the reasons Daddyji had wanted to have club facilities in Simla was his love of cards. He had become part of a card-playing group organized by a Mr. Hayman, of the Railway Board, and renowned for the wealth of its members and for its high stakes. Daddyji had begun to turn more and more from bridge to poker. He had been talked into his first game of straight poker by a member of the Hayman group, and, marvellously, he had won in one night the amount of his bridge earnings in his best month. On a subsequent evening, he had been introduced to stud poker, which was played for much higher stakes than straight poker, and he had lost not only his initial winnings but also many times that amount. Although he never went near stud poker again, he had started going back to the straight-poker table to recoup his losses. Before he knew it, he was playing with a gambler's zeal. Although he was only on a government salary, he thought nothing of risking a month's pay to garner a day's winnings. The Hayman group played at various clubs in Delhi and Simla, where, as a matter of convenience, the card debits and credits were sometimes put on the monthly bills. Rumors of enormous winnings and losses leaked out and were talked about in clubs as far away as Lahore, Bombay, and Calcutta. Once, Sir Joseph Bhore, whose wife was a member of the Fund subcommittee, sent Daddyji a charming letter. "My dear fellow," he wrote. "I do congratulate you for putting tuberculosis on the map, not only with your admirable work during office hours but also with your lucrative extracurricular activities!"

Every evening, while Daddyji played cards at the club, often having a late dinner there, Mamaji waited up patiently for him to come home. If he had won, he would hand her a batch of notes, and she would flush with excitement. If he had lost, the subject wouldn't be broached. She was terrified that he would gamble away her jewels, her saris, the house on Temple Road—everything they owned—but though he sensed her terror, the stakes he played for were so staggering that he could not bring himself to reassure her. Instead, he would absently ask her one or two questions about her day, and she would complain to him about the truculence of a servant, the gossip of a neighbor, the prices in the bazaar.

Mamaji's day had its own routine. She would bathe quickly, put on some clean clothes, sit down on the floor in front of a small ivory statue of Krishna, light a stick of incense, and set it in a dish in front of the statue. She had become a little asthmatic after the birth of her fourth child—a son, named Om Parkash—and her voice was flat. She would chant the same mantras over and over without any self-consciousness—though she would wait until Daddyji had left the house, for he laughed at her rituals as superstition. She knew the ins and outs of every Hindu ceremony and festival, and sometimes she would set forth in a tonga or rickshaw with a basket of sweetmeats and an odd number of rupees—eleven, twenty-one, fifty-one, a hundred and one—for some relative or friend whose son had had a *mundan* (head-shaving ceremony) or whose daughter had been betrothed, married, or delivered of a baby. She spent the rest of her time in household duties; she had a cook, a houseboy, a peon, a washerman, and an ayah to supervise.

Most of all, Mamaji enjoyed playing with the children, who were her life. Promila, being the oldest, was the most sedate, and was Mamaji's favorite; Urmila, being the youngest of the three girls, was noisy and claimed to be Daddyji's favorite, though he insisted that he played no favorites; Nirmila was a sensitive child, interested in everything. All three attended a convent school, and were growing up together like three flowers on a stem. They all had the prominent Mehta nose, long black hair, a graceful carriage, good manners, pleasant voices, and a gift for music. Sometimes, when Daddyji took them on the long drive from Delhi to Simla or from Simla to Lahore, all three of them would sit in the back of the car with Om—"the Prince of Wales," they called him—and sing throughout the journey.

FOR SOME TIME, Daddyji had felt that the Fund subcommittee should be replaced by an independent national tuberculosis organization. "Publicity and propaganda were all well and good when we started," he said at a subcommittee meeting. "But what we need in India

Daddyji and Mamaji, Lahore, 1936

now are sanitariums for the segregation of infectious cases and dispensaries for treatment of non-infectious ones."

He met with sharp opposition from, among others, an Englishman who was the treasurer not only of the subcommittee but also of the Red Cross, and, on top of that, was auditor general of India. "If I didn't know you, Dr. Mehta, I would regard your proposal as a nationalist attempt to subvert British authority," he said. "Nonetheless, I feel I must warn you that you are cutting off a branch of the tree that shelters you."

"Sir, perhaps my branch will grow into a tree bigger than its parent," Daddyji said cockily.

From then on, there was an open feud between the English members of the subcommittee, who wanted to preserve the status quo, and the Indian members, who wanted an independent organization. The chairman at the time, General Sir Cuthbert Sprawson, threw his weight on the English side. The dispute was appealed to the Viceroy. Meanwhile, having served the Fund for six years, Daddyji took six months' leave "ex-India," to which he was entitled before returning to his department in the Punjab.

Daddyji went to London (Mamaji and the children stayed behind, but she accompanied him on a later occasion), and his visit there coincided with a meeting of the Empire Tuberculosis Association; he was named a delegate to the meeting, where he debated with Sir Cuthbert—the head of the Indian delegation—the methods of conquering tuberculosis in India.

"Given the demands on our limited private and public resources in the colonies, publicity and propaganda are the only realistic means of fighting diseases like tuberculosis," Sir Cuthbert said at one point.

"My father used to say, 'Never cross behind a horse lest you be kicked; never cross in front of a boss, lest you be ticked,'" Daddyji said, in his turn. "Despite this wise counsel, I am afraid I have to disagree with my former chief. Public education has gone as far as it can in my country. The time has come to put some muscle into our work. We must open sanitariums and dispensaries for tuberculosis victims and make it a 'notifiable disease,' like smallpox, plague, or cholera. In any case, Sir Cuthbert's idea of propaganda has more application in democratic England, where public opinion precedes the law, than it does in Imperial India, where law precedes public opinion."

Lord Horder, the chairman of the Association meeting, found it extremely distasteful to come down on one side or the other of any controversy, possibly because he expected everyone to muddle through. Daddyji's proposals were therefore ignored in London. In New Delhi, however, they got the nod from the Viceroy.

When Daddyji rejoined his department, one of his first tasks was to supervise the health arrangements for a *mela* (festival) at Kurekshetra. Only an elephant could get through the huge *mela* crowds, and the government commandeered one for Daddyji. Bhabiji, Mamaji, and the children had also come to the *mela*, and on one occasion Daddyji prevailed on Bhabiji to ride with all of them on his elephant. With tears in her eyes, she said, "If only Lalaji were alive, how proud he would feel to see you riding an elephant! It is all exactly as the Brahman of Burkhurdar foretold at your birth."

IX

SONS AND HEIRS

A FTER DADDYJI HAD BUILT HIS HOUSE IN LAHORE, Bhaji Ganga Ram had written to him, "I am getting on in years, and I want to have a place of my own in Lahore for retirement." At the same time, Bhabiji had mentioned to Daddyji that she, too, was eager to have a little house of her own, and that Daulat Ram, who by now had two daughters and a son, should also have a house in Lahore. As it happened, a big plot of land across Temple Road from Daddyji's house was for sale, and was going cheap; because of the worldwide depression, the price of land everywhere had fallen. With the help of loans and savings, the family bought the land jointly and divided it up, and in due course Bhabiji, Daulat Ram, Raj Kanwar, Romesh (Lalaji's fifth son), Bhaji Ganga Ram, and Bhaji Ganga Ram's brother-in-law Vidya Rattan all built houses on it, in the pattern of a *mohalla.* Each house was a smaller copy of Daddyji's, and the *mohalla* was christened Mehta Gulli. So, nearly half a century after Lalaji left Nawankote, a better and more prosperous version of the village was brought into being in the middle of the modern city, but, as with the older generation of Mehta brothers, so with the younger: there was considerable disparity between the fortunes of Daddyji, Daulat Ram, Balwant, Raj Kanwar, Romesh, and Krishan (Lalaji's sixth, and youngest, son).

Daulat Ram had grown up in Daddyji's shadow, but he had never considered his position a disadvantage. He referred to himself as Daddyji's understudy, and when Daddyji vacated a post in the department and moved up in the hierarchy, Daulat Ram almost invariably took his place.

Balwant, after serving as a tailor's apprentice, loafed about in Lahore for a year. He was dissatisfied with tailoring, and Daddyji pulled some strings in Montgomery, where he was posted at the time, and got him a job as an apprentice electrician in the district. After he had worked there a few months, he arrived on Daddyji's doorstep and announced, "I've chucked my job." He said that he didn't like an electrician's work, and that anyway he found life in the district dull and provincial—he missed Lahore's crowded bazaars, its noisy streets, and his friends. "My life motto is '*Khaiye kanak chahe bhuggi hovai,/Rahiye Lahore bhanvai jhuggi hovai*' ["Eat wheat even if it is moth-eaten, and live in Lahore, even in a dingy room"]," he said. "So I am going back to live under Bhabiji's umbrella."

Daddyji, knowing Balwant as he did, saw no point in arguing, but after he himself had been transferred to Lahore he didn't like to see Balwant hanging around the house day after day doing nothing, and suggested that he try his hand at another occupation.

"An idle mind is the Devil's workshop," Balwant said accommodatingly.

Daddyji made an arrangement with Jaggat Singh, the proprietor of Lahore's leading chemist's, whereby Jaggat Singh would accept Balwant as a salesman on the understanding that Daddyji would secretly pay Jaggat Singh seventy-five rupees a month, and Jaggat Singh would give the money to Balwant as wages. Balwant came home after a few months at his job and told Daddyji, "My heart is not in it."

"In what?" Daddyji asked him.

"In selling soap and toothbrushes and fingernail polish and aspirins. Jaggat Singh himself has told me that pharmacology is not my line."

"Oh, no, not again," Daddyji said to himself, but he let it go at that.

Balwant told Bhabiji, "I'm sure if I had a wife I would be able to settle down to a job. I'd like her to have a sweet tongue and to talk well, though."

"What if you get married and don't settle down?" Bhabiji asked. "How will you support her?"

"My ship will come in," he said. "Remember the lottery ticket I bought?"

Soon after that, a friend told Bhabiji, "I know our dear Balwant is a rolling stone, so he will have difficulty finding a wife worthy of the family. But I may be able to arrange things." Bhabiji's friend suggested one of her poorer relatives, Sheila. Bhabiji went and looked her over, and found her to be a simple, angelic soul, with a thin, patient face. Balwant and the girl were married.

"I think my true bent is for tailoring," Balwant now said to Daddyji. "If I only had my own shop, I know I would do very well." Daddyji rented Balwant a shop, stocked it with bolts of silk, wool, and cotton, and bought him a new Singer sewing machine. The new establishment happened to be opposite the bungalow of the very registrar whom Balwant had tried to influence through the notorious barber, so Daddyji named it University Tailors. It was an immediate success; students, professors—indeed, the registrar himself —patronized it. The new-found prosperity was too much for Balwant. He hired an assistant, Mohan, and retired to the back part of his shop, where he tried to re-create the pleasure den of his college days. He smoked, chewed *pan*, relayed college gossip, and played poker. He lost interest in the shop, and it went by default to Mohan, who took over Balwant's obligations along with the goodwill and went on to build up a thriving business.

Balwant by this time was a father several times over, and Bhabiji gave him the family house in Pattoki, which Lalaji had left to her. Reluctantly, he went to Pattoki, where he lived for a while on what his two older brothers contributed. He didn't like his life there any more than he had liked his life in Montgomery, and in time he sold the Pattoki house and was back in Lahore, living with Bhabiji in Mehta Gulli. Bhabiji used to say, *"Tutiyan bahin gal noon aundiyan nain"* ("Broken arms always cling round your neck").

Raj Kanwar passed his B.A. on the second try. He came to Daddyji with the good news, and said, "I want to join the police."

"Lalaji always said, 'I wouldn't let my dog be a policeman,' " Daddyji said. He reminded Raj Kanwar that Lalaji had believed the police to be much worse than the criminals they hunted; in the course of his work, he had seen sub-inspectors at police stations extorting money or confessions from the prisoners by unspeakable tortures. "It's no place for a boy from a good family," Daddyji said.

Raj Kanwar insisted, however, that he was suited for nothing else.

That evening, Daddyji chanced to be introduced to John Ewart, the deputy inspector general of police for the Central Range of the Punjab. Raj Kanwar was on Daddyji's mind, and he told Mr. Ewart the story of the nawab of Tavistock Square and the payoff of the London bobby. "What moral would you draw from the character of the bobby, sir?" he asked.

"If someone had been actually hurt by the bottle, and if your nawab had still gone unpunished, then one would have cause to complain," Mr. Ewart said thoughtfully. "I think that, as it was, the bobby was considerate and helpful. One mustn't overlook how promptly he appeared at the scene of the accident, or the courteous manner in which he discharged his duty. After all, he had to climb up all those stairs and walk into a room that, for all he knew, harbored a dangerous drunkard. The little pocket money he collected from all of you might be considered just compensation for his efforts."

Daddyji and Mr. Ewart had a good laugh together, and they became friends. Thanks to Mr. Ewart, Raj Kanwar was taken into the police as a sub-inspector. "I'm glad to have such a strong boy from such a good family in the force," Mr. Ewart told Daddyji. "I'm sure he'll get quick promotions, and rise to the position of inspector. Possibly he'll even retire as a superintendent of police."

Raj Kanwar was put in charge of a succession of police stations in the Punjab, and quickly made a name for himself in the force for his skill in intramural sports and for his hot temper, which often boiled over into quarrels with his colleagues. As it turned out, he married a small, spunky, equally spirited lady from Lahore, named Janki, who was known in her *mohalla* for her tart tongue; people used to step aside when she flared her nostrils in preparation for a verbal joust.

After eleven years' service, Raj Kanwar, instead of being promoted, was superseded. When he heard of this, he marched into his superior's office, gave him a good tongue-lashing, and tendered his resignation. He came to Daddyji and told him that he was going back to the university to take a law degree, even though by now he was the father of three.

Daddyji was skeptical. Could Raj Kanwar, the indifferent student who had once failed his B.A., really settle down to studying, especially after having been out in the world for so many years?

"My wife, my children, and I are prepared to eat unbuttered bread for as long as it takes me to get through the university," Raj Kanwar said. "Buttered bread and chicken will come in their own good time."

Daddyji wished him well.

Raj Kanwar surprised everybody by getting his law degree in three years and setting himself up as a criminal lawyer. His knowledge of the methods and practices of the police, his contacts in the department, and his police experience with criminals helped to make him a great success.

Romesh spent some time at Government College, won a national competition for a place in an engineering college, and went on to graduate from that college with distinction. He started working as an independent architect in Lahore, with an office on the Mall, and built up a flourishing practice.

One day, he walked into Bhabiji's room—she had turned over her house in Mehta Gulli to Balwant and his family and was living with Romesh—and said, "Will you give your blessing to my marriage?"

She was sitting on her bed in front of her spinning wheel, repeating the name of Ram to the hum of the wheel. Without looking up, she replied that of course she would bless his marriage—after all, he was one of the most eligible bachelors in Lahore, with a house of his own, not to mention a new car, which he had just bought.

"She's upstairs," he said sheepishly.

"Who's upstairs?" she asked, without stopping her work.

"My wife, Savitri," he said.

The news was so unexpected and so confusing that it took her half an hour just to grasp the fact that Romesh, on one of his trips to Bombay, had fallen in love with a Christian girl and had married her secretly.

"Why couldn't you have given me a chance to find you a wife from our own caste and community?" Bhabiji wailed.

"Bhabiji, kings have given up thrones for love," said Romesh. "You've heard about King Edward VIII?"

She stood up. "Where is she? I will not withhold my blessing from a daughter." But as they were going upstairs, she murmured, "A man in Burkhurdar married out of his caste and community, and they used to say of him, '*Ustaryan di mala gal vich pa laee soo,/ Jidhar garden pherega udarhee kategi*' ["He has put a necklace of razors around his neck, and whichever way he turns, it will cut him"]. That couldn't happen to my Romesh."

❦

FROM the very beginning, Daddyji had felt that there was a special bond between him and Krishan. How well he remembered the moment he heard of Krishan's birth, in 1915! He and Daulat Ram had been in the Quadrangle common room, discussing the death of Gopal Krishna Gokhale, the nationalist leader, when a servant brought them the news that Bhabiji had been delivered of another son. "Let's name him Gopal Krishan," Daddyji had said, and the baby had been so named. When Lalaji died, Krishan was only eight. Afterward, he often lived with Mamaji and Daddyji for long stretches, and they always regarded him as their first-born son.

Krishan gave signs of being the most promising of all Lalaji's children and grandchildren; he was handsome, intelligent, artistic, and ambitious. He did well at school, passed his matriculation examination in the first division, won a university merit scholarship to Government College, and stood third in the university intermediate examination. Then, without telling anybody, he sat for an examination for the Indian Military Academy. The Indian Military Academy had recently been established as a concession to nationalistic feelings, and its cadets were to receive the King's Commission—an honor second only to membership in the Indian Civil Service, and one that had previously been reserved for the sons of native princes or of tribal chieftains who had been trained in England at Sandhurst. When the results of the examination were announced, only twenty-two cadets from the entire country were chosen; Krishan was among them, and, in fact, had stood second. He was just seventeen years old.

Soon afterward, while Daddyji was sitting in his office in Simla, Krishan, who was due to leave shortly for the Academy, was shown in. His eyes were red, and around his mouth was a hint of trouble, even as he struggled to maintain a proud, manly expression. "I have failed," he said.

"Failed?"

"In the medical examination for the Military Academy. My chest is a half inch too small for my height, according to the Army's Rules and Regulations."

Daddyji was relieved. When he had first learned of Krishan's intention of going to the Military Academy, he had been alarmed and distressed, for military men led unsettled, hazardous lives, and he had taken it for granted that Krishan would inherit his mantle. But now, looking at Krishan's tremulous expression, Daddyji, in spite of his misgivings, rang up a friend who was an official in the Army Medical Services, and appealed to him for help. The friend drew Daddyji's attention to an obscure footnote in the Army's Rules and Regulations which stated that if a candidate failed his medical examination on a technicality, as Krishan clearly had, he could still go to the Military Academy at his own risk—meaning that he had to take another medical examination at the end of his two-year course, and that if he failed the second time around, he would be denied the King's Commission. Krishan was jubi-

lant; he had no doubt that he would be able to develop
his chest muscles in time.

Just as Krishan had thought, after he passed his
course at the Military Academy he easily got through
his medical examination and received the King's Commission. He chose the Signal Corps, a rather intellectual
branch of the service, and, at the age of twenty, joined
the 4th Battalion of the 19th Hyderabad Regiment as a
lieutenant.

Krishan's letters from the regiment were at first
ebullient: he liked the glamour, the status, and the
camaraderie of an officer's life. Later, they became apprehensive and dejected: he despaired of his future in
the Army. In one letter, he wrote, "I don't think I'll
ever be confirmed or promoted. My colonel says I'm
not fit to be a soldier; he thinks I should have been
a scholar."

Daddyji dismissed Krishan's worries as the natural
anxieties of a young man starting a career, but he had
cause to think of them when, on his way back from his
leave in England, he discovered that one of his fellow-
passengers on the ship was Sir Ivo Vesey, the Chief of
General Staff for India. Recognizing Sir Ivo's poten-
tial importance to Krishan's future, Daddyji cultivated
him—carefully avoiding any mention of a brother in
the armed services.

When Daddyji reached home, he arranged to go
with Krishan to Simla, where Sir Ivo was stationed,
and meet him as if by chance during his daily walk
along the Mall.

Krishan looked every inch a soldier—he was tall
and broad-shouldered, and, though he was on leave,

Daddyji had made certain he was in uniform—and something that was just as striking about him was that he bore a strong resemblance to Daddyji.

Sir Ivo looked Krishan up and down, and exclaimed, "Why, Dr. Mehta, you have an officer in the family! I don't remember your telling me that."

"My brother, Sir Ivo," Daddyji said, with a broad grin and a twinkle. "A chip off the old block."

"I'm more pleased than I can say," said Sir Ivo. He engaged Krishan in conversation, and seemed impressed by his young comrade-in-arms. "I will be coming to Hyderabad for an inspection next month, and I'll look out for you then. Give my compliments to your colonel." He turned to Daddyji. "Dr. Mehta, he's a credit to you and the country."

Once the colonel heard that the family of his young lieutenant was on a social footing with the Chief of General Staff, Krishan never had to look back, especially since he was dedicated to the Army and was determined to do well. He was confirmed and was promoted to the rank of captain.

At the outbreak of the Second World War, his regiment was sent to Singapore. The flavor of his letters was very different now; they were chatty, self-confident, curious, and contented. Once, he wrote, "A brother officer and I took a couple of girls who were visiting here from the United States to a dinner dance last night. It was quite a success. I've joined the local golf club, and today I went looking for a set of clubs—they were quite expensive. How I miss you and Lahore! I wish I were there now. We could go and play tennis or bridge at the club, or go to the cinema, or just sit at home and talk." On another occasion, when Daddyji was visiting Rawalpindi, Krishan wrote, "You must be reviving your old friendship with persons and places in Pindi. My first visit there with you, when I was seven, I still remember very vividly. The first drive from the station in your horse carriage, the rides to Topi Park, gramophone records—all these and many other pictures are stored away in my mind. I remember Tika Ram, and I can picture quite clearly your two-story house, with its courtyard in the center—we on one side, and Bhaji Ganga Ram and Chhoti Bhabiji on the other. I wonder sometimes if it is a good thing to have such a vivid memory of the past. I can live almost all the years of my life again in my memory. Government College Hostel, the house in Little Lane, Murree, Montgomery—I can see all these places any time I want to. I hope you are keeping up your contacts with the Army. You will find a very large number of senior officers in Pindi. Do make friends with them. You will find they are generally very fond of tennis and bridge, and, once their reserve is broken down, they are good friends, too."

Krishan had taken with him to Singapore tubes of paint, some paintbrushes, and a camera, in order to paint and photograph the Malayan jungle, and in a number of his letters he spoke of the strange flora and fauna and of how he was learning to identify them with the help of local guides. Once, he mentioned that he would be back home in a year or so to attend a course at the Staff College at Quetta, by which time he hoped to be an expert woodsman. Within a few months, however, the Japanese entered the war. Krishan found less and less time to write, and he could do little more than hint at the preparations the British had made for the defense of Singapore Island and its fortress, saying merely that the garrison, if attacked, should be able to give a good account of itself. There was nothing to worry about, he said, though for the time being he had to put aside all plans for coming home.

The next news Daddyji had of Krishan was a telegram in January, 1942: "REGRET INFORM YOU CAPTAIN G. K. MEHTA MISSING IN ACTION." From accounts that followed, it appeared that the British had expected the Japanese to attack from the south, from the sea—the guns had been fixed on the harbor—but not for some time. Instead, they had attacked with surprising speed from the north, from the Malay Peninsula, coming overland. Battalion headquarters in Singapore had dispatched orders to Krishan, who was in the jungle on the peninsula with his unit, B Company, to fall back in orderly fashion on Singapore after notifying C Company, which was somewhere in the jungle nearby, to do the same. Krishan sent back word that no one in B Company except him was familiar with the terrain of the jungle. He was therefore taking two men and going in search of C Company. He had not been heard from since, and it was assumed that he had been taken prisoner. That was all anyone knew until August, when the Army relayed a message to Daddyji telling him that a Japanese radio bulletin had just been monitored which said, "One Captain G. K. Mehta has been killed in action, fighting for a cause he didn't understand." But the Army cautioned him against believing the broadcast; it was probably only destructive propaganda, and Krishan might still be alive. In December, however, Daddyji received a letter from K. S. Thimayya, the colonel of Krishan's regiment (who after Independence became Chief of Army Staff of the Indian Army): "It seems that Captain Mehta, on his way back from C Company, saw a lot of enemy movement along the road, and thought this would be a good opportunity to ambush an enemy party. He slipped across to the other side of the road, where his company had been, and found that they had already withdrawn. . . . Captain Mehta and the two men had with them a V.B. gun and a number of hand grenades, so they took up a position alongside the road and commenced using these weapons against enemy tanks and trucks moving down the road. The Japs sent a party through the jungle and, outflanking them, captured Captain Mehta and his two companions. They were then bound to trees and bayoneted to death. This was seen by another sepoy, who escaped and repeated the story on his return. I am afraid this is not very happy news for me to give you, but I feel that you would rather know the truth than stay in uncertainty. I must impress upon you that this account must not be considered official by you. . . . I knew Captain Mehta well, and he was my personal friend. We served together in Malaya for two years, and I can assure you that we are indeed sorry to have lost a good friend and a fine officer. We have anyway the satisfaction that he died with honor, and that his last deeds were done with bravery and leadership of which we are very proud."

Because of the gradual, confused, and unofficial way in which the news about Krishan was disclosed, and because of Daddyji's optimistic nature, he had not been able to bring himself to accept the fact of his brother's death. Long before the action in Singapore, he had wondered what had prompted Krishan to compete for the Military Academy in the first place. Perhaps Krishan had heard Lalaji talk about the Kshatriya warrior stock of the Mehtas—but Krishan had been so young when Lalaji died. Perhaps Krishan had been tantalized by the glory of a King's Commission—but, as far as anyone could tell, he was not more than ordinarily vain. Perhaps, being naturally competitive, Krishan had sat for the examination just to see how well he could score—but then why had he been so shattered when he failed his medical examination? Everything had happened so quickly—he was a commissioned officer before he was twenty—that Daddyji had never discussed Krishan's future with him. Now he was dead at twenty-seven. Daddyji blamed himself for neglecting Krishan, and asked himself what would have happened if he had accepted Krishan's failure in the medical examination, and not tried to find a way around it; if he had accepted the reports of Krishan's being more a scholar than a soldier, and not tried to forward Krishan's career through the use of a little influence. What was there in his own character that always made him want to circumvent destiny, when others resigned themselves unquestioningly to their lot? Had Krishan, perhaps, also overreached himself by attempting to deliver the orders that he was directed to entrust to a subordinate? Some traits did certainly run in the family.

Bhabiji had been told that Krishan was missing in action, but now Daddyji and his brothers could not bring themselves to tell her that Krishan was dead. Their excuse was that her old age should not be haunted by the vision of Krishan bound to the tree and bayoneted. So Bhabiji was told merely that Krishan was a prisoner of war in Japan. When the war ended and all the prisoners came home, the pretense was kept up; she was told that some prisoners were still to be released. Even when, after the war, the Indian subcontinent was partitioned—when Nawankote and Burkhurdar, Multan and Lahore, Mehta Gulli and the house on Temple Road were swallowed up by Pakistan, and when, along with millions of refugees, the Mehta brothers and all their families fled to India and reëstablished themselves, sustained by the hope and enterprise of their forefathers —Bhabiji was still not told the truth about Krishan, and if she suspected the truth, she never showed it. In her last years—she died in 1956, at the age of eighty-five —she was totally blind, and she lived mostly with Mamaji and Daddyji in New Delhi. Whenever she heard an unfamiliar footstep on the veranda, or heard the front door creaking open in the wind, she would start. "Is that my Krishan?" she would say. "He's finally come home—I knew he would."

VED WAS Daddyji's and Mamaji's second son and fifth child. ("Ved" because, though what follows is about my infancy, the memories and feelings described are entirely those of my father. My early memories, as it happens, were blotted out, and, in any case, the story I have been telling belongs not to me but to my father.) He was born in Lahore on the vernal equinox—on Wednesday, the twenty-first of March, 1934, at ten o'clock in the morning. At birth, he weighed nine pounds four ounces. He had a fair complexion, a broad forehead, the prominent Mehta nose, and big brown eyes with long eyelashes. His head was covered with golden curls.

When he was a year old, he and Daddyji used to play a game in the mornings. Daddyji would stick his foot out from under his quilt and into Ved's cot, which was wedged between the beds of Daddyji and Mamaji, and would try to tickle him with his toes. Ved would roll farther and farther away from the invading toes, with explosions of laughter, until he had reached the far edge of his cot. Then Daddyji would withdraw his foot, and Ved would cautiously creep back again. When Daddyji had put his foot back under his quilt, Ved would come into Daddyji's bed and wait for tea to arrive. Then he would snatch the biscuits off the tea tray.

The only time anyone can remember Ved's being unhappy in those days was during his *mundan*, which was held in Lahore on a wintry day when he was a year and a half old. Promila, Nirmila, Urmila, and Om, along with many other relatives, young and old, sat expectantly on the floor in the drawing room, dressed in their best knee socks and turbans, or ribbons and saris. They were waiting to throw rice, myrrh, and frankincense into the sacrificial fire just lit by the Brahman. The offerings were growing sticky in their hands, and the barber had been standing for some time with his straight razor at the ready, but no one seemed to be able to get Ved under control.

Sensing imminent danger, he flailed about in Mamaji's arms, kicking and squirming, shrieking and bellowing at the sight of the barber. Mamaji tried to soothe him with sweetmeats and kisses, but he pushed them away.

Reluctantly, Daddyji took Ved, and, suppressing whatever distaste he felt for the ceremony, he pinned Ved against his chest while the barber, with rapid strokes, shaved off all Ved's silky baby curls.

Everyone hurled his offerings into the fire with relief.

Mamaji quickly tied a pink silk turban over Ved's shaven head, and the Brahman put a saffron religious mark on his forehead and chanted some mantras. Sweetmeats—the *prashad*—were distributed, with savories, tea, milk, and lemonade. The boy was now formally christened Ved Parkash, and he was made to sit for a photograph.

A year later, Daddyji, Mamaji, Ved, and Usha, the fourth daughter and sixth child, who had just been born, were travelling by car from Lahore to Gujrat, where Daddyji had been posted as district health officer after his return from leave in England. Gujrat lay seventy miles northeast of Lahore on the Grand Trunk Road. It was late afternoon, the road was crowded with bullock carts and lorries, the air was hot and dusty, and Daddyji was anxious to get to Gujrat before dark. Ved was sitting in Mamaji's lap, and the baby slept in a basket in the back seat; the other children were all away at boarding school.

As the car wove in and out of the traffic, Ved seized the steering wheel.

Normally, Daddyji would have taken Ved on his

Ved, Head-Shaving Ceremony, 1935

lap, but instead he yanked Ved's hand away. Ved reached out for the wheel again, and Daddyji slapped his fingers.

Ved started screaming.

"Quiet!" Daddyji said sharply.

Mamaji held Ved against her and tried to distract him by showing him the shiny handle of the side window. Though generally good-tempered, Ved was used to having his own way; he was stubborn and precocious, quick to take injury. He went on howling.

Daddyji never knew what came over him, but he slammed on the brakes, jumped out of the car, came around to Mamaji's side, and threw open the door.

"He'll be all right, dear," Mamaji said. "It's all right."

"I know what I'm doing," Daddyji said, and he wrenched Ved out of her arms. As she looked on helplessly, Daddyji set Ved down on the roadside and got back into the car.

Ved sat on the shoulder of the road, his legs outstretched and his arms raised over his head, his body tensed for a scream, which he seemed too frightened to expel.

Daddyji moved the car ahead a few yards. He looked at Mamaji out of the corner of his eye and saw that she was weeping silently, and suddenly his rage dissolved. He stopped the car, ran back to Ved—who, at the sight of rescue, began to bawl—and picked him up and fondled him. Ved's screams subsided, Daddyji gave him to Mamaji, and they drove on.

Gujrat turned out to be a very pleasant posting. Daddyji, Mamaji, Ved, and the baby lived in a government bungalow with an airy veranda and lots of big windows. The bungalow was on a quiet road, and all around were the houses of other government officers, with wide lawns and shady trees; nearby were the grass tennis courts of the Gujrat Club. Life in Gujrat was so amiably comfortable that Daddyji's immediate superior, the assistant director of public health for the division, evaluated the work of his subordinates by totting up the number of nights they spent away on tour in the district. Daddyji wanted to be in his superior's good books, because, among other things, he himself stood an excellent chance of being promoted to an assistant directorship, and so he tried to go on tour as much as possible. It happened, however, that in the month of December—the year was 1937—he had not left Gujrat for more than seven days all told, when he should have been away twice as much. Accordingly, in January he went on a longish tour, taking Mamaji, Ved, and the baby in the car with him.

Their first stop was at a dak bungalow beside a canal six miles from Dinga, a town at the foot of the Himalayas. Daddyji, after they had eaten lunch, took the car and went up-country for a quick inspection of some villages, to check whether all the inhabitants had been vaccinated against smallpox.

A couple of hours passed, and since he still hadn't returned, Mamaji decided to leave the baby with a servant, go out for a walk with Ved, meet Daddyji on the road, and drive back with him. There were two dirt roads—one along the lower bank of the canal, one along the upper bank. Daddyji had gone by the upper road, and that was the road Mamaji and Ved took.

A cold wind was sweeping down from the hills, but they walked on, expecting to see Daddyji's car appear at any moment.

When they had gone about a mile and a half and there was still no sign of the car, Mamaji and Ved crossed the canal by a footbridge and started back on the lower road, which was somewhat sheltered.

When they reached the dak bungalow, they found Daddyji there. "Where have you been?" he asked.

Mamaji told him.

"I must have just missed you." He had taken the upper road and had arrived half an hour before.

Mamaji put a thick sweater on Ved, and he drank a cup of hot milk while Mamaji and Daddyji had their tea. Afterward, Ved and Daddyji went out to play on the lawn, taking with them a child's hockey stick and a ball.

They played hockey for a little while and, when Ved tired of that, hide-and-seek. There were shrubs bordering the lawn, and Ved would hide behind them. Daddyji would pretend not to know where, and call out to Mamaji, "Shanti, have you seen Ved anywhere?"

"No, dear, I haven't, but I think he was just here," she would answer from inside the dak bungalow.

Daddyji would walk about the lawn whistling to himself, stop in front of the shrubbery where Ved was hiding, and part it, and Ved would run out, laughing, and disappear behind another shrub.

At dinner, Ved didn't want to eat. Mamaji coaxed him to take a few spoonfuls of mutton curry and rice, and he vomited. She took him to the bedroom they were all sharing, and tucked him in, and he fell asleep.

She got up in the middle of the night and felt Ved's forehead. He was very feverish. She woke Daddyji, and they took Ved's temperature. It was a hundred and five degrees. She sat up with Ved all night, and Daddyji didn't go out on his inspection the next day. They took Ved's temperature periodically, and it remained the same.

In the late afternoon, Daddyji decided to cut his tour short, and they drove back to Gujrat. Instead of going home, they went straight to the hospital. A specimen of Ved's blood was taken, and they consulted the assistant civil surgeon, Dr. Bhatia—a family friend, who lived in the hospital compound.

He examined Ved thoroughly, and told Daddyji, "I don't want to jump to any conclusions, but it might be a severe case of pneumonia. We'll know more when we get the blood report tomorrow morning."

Daddyji, when any of his children or his wife became ill, always disqualified himself from the case and submitted to the judgment of other doctors. But now he asked if it wouldn't be a good idea to put Ved on Prontosil Rubrum, a German "wonder drug," which had just been introduced into India and was recommended for infectious fevers. "It might bring down the fever," he said.

Dr. Bhatia concurred.

They went home, and during that night Mamaji and Daddyji stayed up alternately, administering doses of Prontosil, taking Ved's temperature, and watching for symptoms of pneumonia. Though he had some difficulty in breathing, his chest remained clear, and by morning his temperature had dropped to a hundred and one.

A peon arrived from the hospital with the results of Ved's blood test. Looking at them, Daddyji began to suspect cerebrospinal meningitis, even though its symptoms—high fever and nausea—had disappeared overnight. Had the Prontosil perhaps masked them?

Daddyji sent a note to Dr. Bhatia telling him of his suspicions and asking him to come over right away with a trocar and cannula from the hospital, so that they could perform a lumbar puncture. The lumbar puncture would both determine whether Ved had meningitis and, if so, immediately lessen the pressure of the cerebrospinal fluid on the brain. He then sent a note to Dr. Debru, the civil surgeon and the senior man of Gujrat medicine, asking him if he could stop by and examine Ved.

Dr. Bhatia arrived, and agreed about the suspicion of meningitis, and he and Daddyji started making preparations for the lumbar puncture without waiting for Dr. Debru. They were sterilizing the surgical instruments when Dr. Debru walked in.

Dr. Debru looked Ved over—he was sitting up in bed and drinking milk—while Dr. Bhatia filled his superior in on the case history so far.

"There is no stiffness in the neck or back," Dr. Debru said, "and when have you heard of a meningitis patient sitting up and drinking milk? By this time, he would be in a feverish coma. He couldn't possibly have meningitis."

Daddyji, who was standing by the side of Ved's

bed, said hesitantly, "He is generally a very healthy child, and Prontosil could have brought down the fever and relieved the stiffness in the spine."

"You should take him off Prontosil immediately," the senior man said. "These new drugs can do as much harm as good. Prontosil's a two-edged sword."

The remark had its intended effect. Daddyji discontinued the treatment with Prontosil and dropped the idea of the lumbar puncture as well.

He went to his office, and returned in the late afternoon. Without taking off his hat or coat, he went to see Ved.

"Which hat do I have on my head?" he asked. He owned a brown felt hat and a gray felt hat, and he was wearing the gray one.

Ved raised himself up and looked hard at Daddyji. "I can't tell," he said, and he fell back on the pillow.

Daddyji went out to the pantry, where Mamaji was washing the thermometer. "Ved couldn't tell which hat I was wearing," he said. "Meningitis often affects the eyes."

"It's not good to think bad thoughts," she said. "Anyway, his temperature has stayed at a hundred and one."

"I would like to get an expert opinion," Daddyji said. "I'm going to telephone Daulat Ram in Lahore to see if he can get a specialist." He put through a trunk call to the Epidemiological Bureau in Lahore, where Daulat Ram had his office.

"Dr. D. R. Mehta is not in at present," said a voice at the other end of the line.

"Where is he?"

"He is attending a medical fair at the Exhibition Grounds."

"Please find him, and tell him that his elder brother wants to speak to him urgently."

But it was several hours before Daddyji finally spoke to Daulat Ram, who told him that it would be difficult to get a specialist to come to Gujrat quickly, and that instead he should drive Ved to Lahore. "Anyhow, if his temperature has come down to a hundred and one, he seems to be getting better," Daulat Ram said.

The commissioner for the division, Mr. Cuthbert King, who was coming on tour from Rawalpindi, was expected to arrive in Gujrat that evening. Daddyji, whose promotion to an assistant directorship was still pending, was anxious to please him, and had previously arranged a tennis party for him at the club, with the deputy commissioner, E. P. Moon, and the superintendent of police, Rai Sahib Chunni Lal Kapoor. After talking to Daulat Ram, Daddyji put off going to Lahore until the next day, and went out to the club, where the four passed the evening playing doubles.

The next morning, Daddyji, realizing that too much movement might be dangerous for Ved, borrowed the car of the Rai Sahib, which was the biggest car in Gujrat, so that Ved could ride to Lahore lying down on the back seat. Rai Sahib lent his driver along with the car, so Mamaji rode in back with Ved, while Daddyji followed in his car with the baby, and they drove slowly to a hospital in Lahore, where Daulat Ram had made all the arrangements. A neurosurgeon from the military, Dr. Luthra, who had been involved in controlling a meningitis epidemic in the Army, was waiting.

"It looks to me like a very bad case of cerebrospinal meningitis," the doctor said after looking at Ved's eyes; he had begun to squint. "I wish you had performed the lumbar puncture when you first thought of it."

Within minutes, Dr. Luthra was performing a lumbar puncture. As Daddyji stood there at Ved's bedside, watching the surgeon put the needle to the small of the back, where the little bones showed through the skin—something he himself was not emotionally equipped to do—he had a premonition of death. He thought how different the outcome might have been if he had gone through with the lumbar puncture earlier, if he had not deferred to Dr. Debru, if he had not discontinued the Prontosil, which had been proved effective against meningitis. Bitterness was not in his nature—he automatically made allowances for others— but anger was. He was furious with himself for the tour to Dinga and for the tennis game at the club, both done for the sake of advancement. Yet had he ever had a choice in any of it? There were the children to raise and educate, and one's superiors were everything. But then he saw the child sitting by the roadside, arms outstretched, too frightened to cry out, and he was certain he had always been the agent of his actions. In fact, from his school days he had taken pride in repeating, "I am the master of my fate."

"What are his chances?" he now asked.

"I think we'll be able to save his life," Dr. Luthra said. "As for the rest, no one can say. Brain damage is what is most common in these cases."

Daddyji now watched the cloudy fluid rush out from Ved's spine; the pressure had obviously been building up for several days. Dr. Luthra drew over seventy cubic centimetres of fluid. Ved's brain—or, at the very least, his eyes—had certainly been damaged.

Ved was squinting worse than before, and two ophthalmologists were called in for consultation. They said that the optic nerves had probably been damaged long since, but, on the off chance that partial eyesight might be saved, they recommended that atropine be put regularly in his eyes to keep the pupils dilated.

As a man, Daddyji had cried only once—at the news of Lalaji's death, almost fifteen years earlier. He now broke down again and cried helplessly.

During the night, Daddyji inexplicably developed a high fever, with severe chills. He became delirious and muttered incoherently.

Mamaji sat by his pillow, distraught, understanding nothing of what he said. She shook down the thermometer to normal for him and caught herself putting it in her own mouth.

In the morning, Daddyji got up in a daze (they had spent the night in a hospital room adjoining Ved's) and mechanically ransacked the Temple Road house for Lalaji's letters, diaries, and account books—the written records of the family's history and quick rise. In those papers Lalaji had off and on discussed members of the family with candor, dwelling on their shortcomings and on the hardship of his humiliating job, and Daddyji now got them all together and burned them. He felt he was going to die, and he didn't want any mean record to survive him.

Ved's illness lasted two months. His case was so acute that his spine was tapped morning and evening, and in the beginning as much as fifty or sixty cubic centimetres of cerebrospinal fluid was drawn at each puncture. The source of his infection was never traced, for the health authorities were unable to discover a single other case of meningitis in the district. It was therefore supposed that Ved must have been exposed to an undetected carrier and must have been so fatigued by his three-mile walk in the cold wind that he had easily fallen victim to the disease.

The flow of fluid gradually diminished, and Ved's life and his brain were spared. But it was clear when the fever abated that the optic nerves had been irrevocably damaged. He was left totally blind.

IN THIS SUPERSTITIOUS SOCIETY, Daddyji knew, it would be said that the gods had branded Ved with blindness for the misdeeds of his previous life, just as the police still sometimes branded murderers on the forehead with a hot iron. It was taken for granted that blindness, like leprosy, was the lot only of the poor and the cursed. From his work in the health department, Daddyji knew all too well about the lack of educational facilities for the blind. For that matter, Mamaji thought that the blindness of her child, brought on by brain fever, must be the consequence of some misdeed she herself had committed in an earlier incarnation, and she had already set about working toward improvement in her next life by redoubled piety and devotion. In a different way, Daddyji looked to his own past, much as he would have liked to burn it up. He was, however, comforted, at least in respect to the fateful tour and the tennis game, by a letter of sympathy from the deputy commissioner, E. P. Moon, which concluded:

> . . . God doth not need
> Either man's work or his own gifts. Who best
> Bear his mild yoke, they serve him best. . . .
> They also serve who only stand and wait.

DURING VED'S ILLNESS, Daddyji had stayed in Lahore, on leave from the government. He could not bear to return to Gujrat, and he now asked the government for a transfer. His new posting was to the sleepy canal colony of Karnal, where he, Mamaji, Ved, and the baby lived in a small bungalow overlooking a tributary of the river Jumna. There the pattern of Daddyji's old life—of relaxed work at the office, tennis and cards at the club, pleasant tours in the car—gradually reasserted itself. One day in the club, he heard there were schools for the blind in Bombay and Calcutta, and immediately placed advertisements in their leading papers, saying that he had a blind son and was looking for a good school for him. In response to the advertisement, he received a letter from a Ras Mohun Halder, who deplored his countrymen's public indifference toward the blind, noting that in India young children and old men were thrown together in the dormitories and workshops of asylums, while in advanced countries like America there were schools for the blind every bit as good as the schools for the sighted. He finished his letter by saying that he was an Indian Christian; that, although he was sighted, he had spent some time at one of these schools studying teaching methods for the blind; and that he had just taken charge of an American mission school for the blind in Bombay, for which he was appealing for support.

Daddyji immediately wrote back to Mr. Halder, saying that he wished to give Ved such an education as would enable him later to study in America and to lead a normal life.

Soon afterward, Daddyji received a reply from Mr. Halder suggesting that Ved be entered in his school without delay. He said that he, his wife, and his infant daughter lived in the school building, and that Ved could board with them at a cost of seventy-five rupees a month. Mr. Halder himself would give him some instruction.

Daddyji was taken by the idea, even though, after making some inquiries, he discovered that the school was a single shabby building in the industrial slum of Dadar, itself not much more than an asylum for waifs and strays. When he informed Mamaji of his plans, she told him that, of course, he knew best, but she thought it heartless to send a blind child more than a thousand miles away from home and entrust him to the care of strangers, who, for all anyone knew, were rogues and swindlers. "I know he'll be able to see," she said. "Your kind of doctors have made him blind, but my kind of doctors will restore his sight."

"He'd be better off if he were away from your superstitions," he said harshly. He had just found out that she had been taking Ved secretly to practitioners

of native medicine, who gave her false hopes and ridi-
culed all that Daddyji stood for as a man of Western
science. But then he repented of the cruelty with which
he had spoken, and said, "You'll see—everything will
turn out for the best. Lalaji used to say of us, 'Look
where they started, and look where they've reached!'
And who is to say where Ved will end up?"

ONE WINTRY MORNING, Ved, who was not quite five,
was taken to the railway station in Lahore. Bibi Parmeshwari Devi's bachelor son Prakash, who was going
to Bombay to look for a job as a writer for films, was to
accompany him on the train. Ved held on to Mamaji's
neck and wouldn't let go. Daddyji tried to take him
from her by promising him sweetmeats from a vender
who was hawking his wares up and down the platform,
and by talking to him about the whoosh and whistle of
the engine and about the magic surprises of the train
compartment.

Mamaji set him down, and he clung to Daddyji's
legs. He was wearing a bright-yellow satin suit.

"Why can't I go to the same school as my brother?"
he cried.

Daddyji explained to Ved that he had to go to a
special school.

"Then why don't you come with me?" he asked,
between sobs.

Daddyji felt weak. Some time before they had all
left for the station, he had overheard a conversation. An
errand boy had wandered onto the veranda where Ved
was playing, and, not realizing that the child was blind,

had said, "What a pretty yellow suit you have on today!"

"I can't tell," Ved had said. "I'm blind."

"Why don't you tell your father that you're having trouble with your eyes?" the errand boy had said. "He's a doctor-sahib, and he'll make you all better."

"I don't want to hurt him by telling him I can't see," Ved had said.

Now Daddyji heard the whistle—the Frontier Mail was pulling out. He snatched Ved up and handed him, crying, through the window of the compartment to Prakash.

The last words Daddyji said to Ved (and the first words I remember hearing) were "You're a man now."

GLOSSARY

ASHARAFI: monetary unit; equivalent to one guinea

AYAH: nursemaid

BARAT: bridegroom's party

BHABI: elder brother's wife

BHAJI: elder brother

BHANG: hemp intoxicant

BIBI: honorific title for a girl or a woman

BIRI: hand-rolled cigarette

CHAPATTI: unleavened pancake-shaped bread

CHARPOY: light bedframe strung with tape or light rope

CHELA: spiritual disciple; pupil

CHHOTI: little

CHIK: screen blind of finely split bamboo laced with twine

DAK BUNGALOW: house for travellers at a postal station

DHARAMSHALA: shelter for travellers; pilgrims' hostel

DHOTI: loincloth of varying length

DURBAR: prince's court; public levee of prince, governor, or viceroy

EKKA: small one-horse vehicle

GHI: clarified butter

GULLI: narrow street or alleyway

HARI CHHAL: a small green banana

HOOKAH: water-cooled smoking pipe, hubble-bubble

-JI: suffix denoting affection and respect

KAMEEZ: loose shirt

KHASRA: account book

LALA: caste title

MAHARAJA: king (Hindu)

MAHARANI: queen (Hindu)

MANDI: market

MANTRA: Vedic hymn or prayer

MAULVI: learned religious leader (Muslim)

MELA: festival (Hindu)

MOHALLA: a block of houses built around a courtyard; a neighborhood

MUNDAN: head-shaving ceremony

MUNSHI: clerk

NAMASTE: ceremonial greeting (Hindu)

NAUTCH: professional dancing

NAWAB: honorific title for an important or wealthy man (Muslim)

PAN: betel-leaf masticatory

PANDA: one belonging to the Brahman sub-caste of genealogists

PARATHA: fried unleavened wheat bread

PATWARI: petty official, land recorder

PICE: monetary unit—one sixty-fourth of a rupee

PRASHAD: blessed food

PUNKA: fan

PURANAS: Sanskrit sacred poems

PURDAH: curtain; system of secluding women of rank

RAI BAHADUR: title conferred on Indians by the English

RICKSHAW: light, two-wheeled hooded vehicle, drawn by a man or men

RUPEE: basic monetary unit

SADHU: holy man (Hindu)

SAHIB: honorific title for a man

SALAAM: ceremonial greeting (Muslim)

SALWAR: pajama trousers

GLOSSARY

SARANGI: bowed stringed instrument

SARDAR: honorific title for a man (Sikh)

SARI: woman's draped garment

SEPOY: sentry

SITAR: plucked stringed instrument

SOLA TOPI: pith sun helmet

SWAMI: holy man (Hindu)

SYCE: groom

TABLA: hand drum

TANDUR: clay oven; food stall

TONGA: light, two-wheeled, one-horse vehicle

TOPI: hat

-WALLAH: person or thing employed about or concerned with something

ZILLADAR: district administrative officer